AGE OF UNION

DAX DASILVA

IGNITING THE CHANGEMAKER

Age of Union

First Edition
Published in Canada in 2019
By Anteism Books

Author
Dax Dasilva

Art Direction and Design
Baillat Studio

Art Curation
Jean-Sébastien Baillat

Editorial Director
Catherine Métayer

Editors
Sara Smith and Jeremy Young

Proofreaders
Shanti Maharaj and Edwin Janzen

Illustrator
Stéphane Poirier

Director of Public Relations
Bradley Grill

Never Apart Photography
Saad Al-Hakkak
Yasuko Tadokoro

Written contributions
for the following chapters:
Nature: Catherine Métayer
Acts of Union: Mark Mann

Artist Bios
Sky Goodden and Sara Smith

Contributing Artists
Refik Anadol
Neil Krug
Nik Mirus
Bradley G Munkowitz
Benoît Paillé
Tess Roby
Julie Roch-Cuerrier
Florence Yee
Jonathan Zawada

Age of Union ©2019
Dax Dasilva

All Rights Reserved.
No part of this publication may be
reproduced or transmitted in any
form or by any means, electronic
or mechanical, including photocopy,
recording, or any other information
storage or retrieval system, without
prior permission in writing from the
publishers.

A catalogue record for this book is
available from Library and Archives
Canada.

ISBN 978-1-926968-34-6

Printed by Marquis, Montréal.
Bound by Multi-Reliure, Shawinigan,
and BookArt, Montréal.

Typefaces
Du Nord, Playtype™
Tiempo Text, Klim Type Foundry

Paper
Rolland Enviro 70# Smooth

Anteism
6201 Av du Parc #409
Montréal, QC
H2V 4H6, Canada

For information about Anteism's
publications, please visit:
www.anteism.com

Age of Union
Twitter / Instagram
@ageofunion
www.ageofunion.com

The intention of this book is to plant the seed for an Age of Union, igniting the changemaker in every one of us.

That seed contains a call to action and a call for awareness: to prime our world for the coming age, to awaken us for the transformation, to end separation and be *never apart*.

"I used to think that the top environmental problems were biodiversity loss, ecosystem collapse, and climate change.

"I thought that thirty years of good science could address these problems. I was wrong. The top environmental problems are selfishness, greed, and apathy.

"To deal with these we need a cultural and spiritual transformation.

"And we scientists don't know how to do that."

— Gus Speth, American environmental lawyer and advocate

Introduction

A Word from Dax

We each have the power to be a changemaker. This book is about igniting the flame within. My journey has taught me that we can find our purpose in being our authentic selves and learning to be a force for the greater good. We tend to experience the world through both its natural and manufactured separations. But we must overcome these separations and collectively move toward something new. I want to show that it's possible to reframe our understanding of the world in terms of union, or *unseparation*, so that we can become the impactful changemakers that the world needs now.

A few months before opening the Never Apart Centre in Montréal in 2015, I wrote a manifesto for the project—the progenitor of this book, *Age of Union*. I poured my intention for multi-faceted unity across humanity, society, and nature into its words. I didn't know how the cultural centre would take shape, or what paths it might lead us down—I only knew I wanted to make a difference.

The core idea of the Centre was to create social change and transformation, but also to bring forth spiritual awareness through the powerful modes of culture. We wanted to do what the words "Never Apart" suggested: bring an end to separation. We believed that by exploring culture we could help remove the barriers between people of different backgrounds and perspectives and begin breaking down our separation from nature to better understand our place in this world.

In the sections that follow, I will share my background as both the founder of Never Apart and the founder and CEO of the tech company Lightspeed. You'll get to know me as a spiritually and environmentally interested person. I'll also share with you some details about my own journey, as well as my vision, to provide a clearer understanding of the place this book comes from: a place of belief that humanity can turn things around; that societal division and environmental degradation are not the only paths forward on our planet; and that we can make positive change if we set the right intentions and put them into action.

READING AGE OF UNION

Age of Union is a personal vision, one that you are invited to connect with in any way that resonates with you. At times, its language may read like a directive; at others, like poetry. In some areas, the writing will be steeped in mystical thought; elsewhere, it will be grounded in scientific study. I invite you to enjoy the read for the creative, artistic, and spiritual journey through which it will walk you.

My intention is to inspire and be inclusive, and to fuel a passion for change, transformative action, and unity. Many are concerned for our collective future. Many are concerned for the animals and ecosystems that enrich our world and sustain our ability to live on this planet. Many wonder if spiritual knowledge, balanced by the scientific understandings and achievements of our species, can help us solve the world's problems. I share these concerns and thoughts. I feel we can only move forward by making efforts to unite our paths and focus on finding solutions.

Spiritual exploration embraces and celebrates humanity's journey. It teaches us that our journey can be at once remembered and renewed by this generation. It can help us walk this challenging road toward union together. Spiritual and mystical traditions show us how, as a people, we have reached toward that which seemed beyond all understanding. We can learn from traditions that, in today's world, can be reclaimed with modern application. Their absence has left us feeling disconnected and lacking meaning or purpose in our actions.

A FRAMEWORK FOR CHANGE

Age of Union presents a vision for a time when we've reconciled the disconnections that have happened along our journey and *unseparated* the barriers to repair and reconnect the world. It takes courage to open one's heart, but when we do, we open a space that can be filled with the strength to be leaders in our own destined capacity, to connect with one another through different expressions of culture, to celebrate the teachings of our diversity, to protect nature as we move into an era of guardianship, and to find the spiritual in the everyday. This is to know the joy of purpose.

17/05/16
15:08:47

Age of Union

Beginnings

THE PERSONAL WALK

The wealth of experience I gained from leading my tech company, Lightspeed, through nearly a decade and a half of hyper-growth has played an important part in my personal walk. At Lightspeed, we have focused on culture just as much as code. I feel an enormous sense of responsibility to ensure that the company and its people reach their full potential. With high aspirations, I have taken risks that have been founded on a spiritual base. This was a deep source of strength when I faced cardinal points in our journey. I learned to trust in this elemental source of growth. And I have been entrusted with a company where the bounty of that faith was revealed in a unique ability to survive, reinvent, and thrive.

While startup life shaped an important part of me, I felt a growing need to explore other parts of myself: my cultural, spiritual, and environmental leanings.

Even after hours of talking shop, my father never ended one of our phone calls without reminding me that I was not responsible alone for the success of my company. He was right. Letting go and trusting in higher guidance would result in outcomes for Lightspeed that I could not have conceived of on my own. The company grew far beyond my expectations and, early on, I stopped having preconceptions about our limitations. I led with resilience, but I also gave the company over to that far greater force. Year upon year, the company would rise through challenges to reach new heights.

Both sides of my family are originally from Goa, a small state on the west coast of India. Portuguese spice traders colonized the region in the 16th century, before the British Empire, and they maintained their hold on the territory for nearly 450 years, until its annexation by India in 1961. As such, the Portuguese exerted a strong influence on Goan culture, converting the local people to Catholicism and giving them Portuguese family names such as ours, *da Silva*, meaning *of the forest*. My father's family, originally of the Brahman priestly Hindu caste, continued the religious tradition of the family as Catholic priests, nuns, and caretakers of the village chapel. In the 1920s, my grandparents' generation resettled in Uganda to help build the civil service in the new British colony. They thrived until the country became unstable and unsafe in 1971, when military dictator Idi Amin provoked a bloody civil war. My parents came to Canada in 1972 as refugees—my father, age 25 at the time, and my mother, just 19. Prime Minister Pierre Elliott Trudeau chartered planes to bring the English-speaking, educated immigrants from Uganda to an army base in Montréal. There they found the destination cities of their relatives already in Canada on message boards. My parents chose to settle in Vancouver, where they married and where my sister and I were born just a few years later.

I was an artistic, academic child from a family of entrepreneurs, creatives, and intellectuals—spiritual, good-hearted, and generous people. As a kid, I loved to paint and draw, and, nurtured by a loving and scholastic mother, had a strong run in school, cultivating a vivid imagination. I entered the tech world when my father, a communications director and graphic designer, brought home a Mac.

I became obsessed with the crossover between the liberal arts, design, and tech that this new kind of computer represented. I turned my interest in user interface design into learning programming, to bring my interface designs to life. All through my teens and early twenties, I built a software development and tech support practice, combining my love for creation with my enjoyment of learning about people.

I came out as a gay man in my teens in the early 1990s. I would make the Friday-night bus rides from the suburbs of Richmond to the Vancouver Gay and Lesbian Centre, or GLC as it was called, for the weekly youth group meeting. Arriving there at 14 years old, it would be years before people my own age would start attending. I made supportive friendships, met with counsellors, accessed a library of LGBTQ books, and engaged in discussions that helped me understand that being gay was an experience shared by many others, and that while it was different, it was also both normal and special. Being gay was less understood at the football-oriented, all-boys, Irish Catholic high school I attended, and my coming out to friends in Grade 9 was met with a mixed reception. I became more muted about my sexuality until Grade 11, when it became broadly known and accepted as part of who I was by friends and fellow students, many of whom later came out as gay themselves. They have remained close friends throughout my life.

Coming out to my parents at age 18 meant an adjustment to their understanding of what my future would hold, but that understanding grew over time—their love and acceptance never wavered. My father, though emotional when I first told him, accepted my coming out and made a deal with me to engage in a form of cross-education: he would visit the GLC if I visited and listened to the perspective of a Christian prayer group. He had been on a spiritual journey after going through a difficult period in his life, and spirituality was always a topic of exploration and common ground between us. This exchange, through the people and literature of the GLC, resulted in my father realizing the positive connection he had with gay people in his life and that some of his closest friends and colleagues were part of the LGBTQ community. In these late teenage years, I was also "adopted" into the club scene by an Indonesian transgender woman who became a second maternal figure in my life, and who protected me and others my age from negative influences.

Around the same period of time, I enlisted in the environmentalist battle to save the old-growth forests of British Columbia. At 17, I drove to the west coast of Vancouver Island to protest at Clayoquot Sound. Groves of thousand-year-old trees, which stood like nature's cathedrals, were to be destroyed by clear-cut. Our protests won the preservation of those forests. Yet on the journey to Clayoquot I had seen the dead, grey, clear-cut valleys that previous generations had not saved. These images of man-made moonscapes on earth have never left my mind.

At the University of British Columbia, my early career in technology directed me into computer science. However, by the end of the first year, I realized that four years of statistics, calculus, and engineering were not my path. After taking a year off, I returned to UBC to study art history and religious studies, following my heart to explore my cultural and spiritual interests. While studying the Abrahamic faiths of Judaism, Christianity, and Islam, I found myself drawn to the journey and covenant of the Jewish people, and in my first Judaic studies class, I felt a rush of wind inside as the professor read the opening lines of Genesis in Hebrew—a literal sensation of the words *ruach adonai*.[1] I began to explore deeply as I found roots for my personal spiritual growth in Judaism's rich mystical tradition, a thread that can be found woven throughout this book.

I transitioned my tech consulting business into jobs that spanned from Vancouver to Montréal after my move to this city in 2001 at age 24. Montréal's cultural vibrancy, diversity, and open-mindedness resonated with how I wanted to live my life; it was an inspiring, cosmopolitan city where I would find the fertile ground to challenge myself socially and professionally. After a layoff from a company where I developed software during my early years in the city, I considered what my next steps would be. My love of the culture of Montréal, as well as my experience of the underground music scene, led me to follow some personal ambitions to learn how to produce electronic music and start writing, inspired by the mysticism I was studying. I often look back at this transitional period as being the spark that would eventually conceive Never Apart—an attempt to combine the cultural with the spiritual and to find new ways to connect new audiences with both.

At this juncture in 2005, two things happened in tandem. I began building the enterprise that would become Lightspeed, and I made a conversion to Judaism. I had come to two very foundational turning points that would determine the course of my life's journey for the next decade. A company was born on a deepening faith that could weather the rigours and challenges of building and leading a startup. And my faith was enriched with the life experiences and diversity of people that running one of Canada's fastest-growing companies would allow me to learn from.

From the ages of 28 to 38, I set aside the idea of combining the cultural and spiritual in a new project. I trusted in my journey of putting all of myself into building Lightspeed as well as investing in my personal growth. Both progressed hand in hand, infusing the company with the best of what the spiritual brought out of me, the trials and triumphs of the company preparing me to lead in broader ways in the future.

GROWING AT LIGHTSPEED

Lightspeed grew rapidly from the start, and today employs over seven hundred bright minds across eight cities.[2] The company did not take outside investment for our first seven years, and the building in the Mile-Ex neighbourhood, our fourth office (which would become the Never Apart cultural centre years later), would be our last purchase before we raised nearly $300 million in funding, from investors in Silicon Valley and Québec, between 2012 and 2017. We grew the company into an international force

[1] Hebrew expression for the "wind of God."
[2] Figures are from 2019.

for cloud-based point-of-sale and e-commerce software, our mission being to even the playing field for independent small and medium-sized business owners and help them be more data-driven and competitive. We wanted to keep cities unique and thriving by providing tools for local entrepreneurs that were up against both the big chains and the e-commerce giants of the world.

When Lightspeed outgrew 7049 St-Urbain in 2015 and we began preparing for our move to the Gare Viger, a 120-year-old restored railway hotel that lay east of Old Montréal, the question of what to do with the Mile-Ex building presented itself. I sensed this was an opportunity to fulfill a long-held dream. At this point, Lightspeed was celebrating its 10-year anniversary and, truthfully, 10 years of building a startup with the roller coaster of stresses and successes that comes with being the CEO and shepherd of this growing family had left me burnt out. It also left me thinking about whether I was the right person to take the company to its next stage and if the other things I wanted to do with my life's experience would ever be realized.

Leading Lightspeed challenged me in ways I could never have imagined: managing teams, executives, technology, marketing, design, finance, and investors as well as handling crises, launching products and offices, staving off competitors, adapting to new market conditions, and rapidly transforming consumer behaviour—reinventing my role year upon year to best serve our people and mission. I built the original software and then evolved as a leader through every stage of the company.

We chose to build Lightspeed on the strengths of diversity and inclusion. We hired brilliant people. And we established teams in places with cultures as diverse as Montréal, Amsterdam, Ghent, New York, London, and the U.S. west coast, which themselves revealed subcultures in every department of engineering, sales, support, and operations. Somehow, we have still been able to find unity on our mission—a celebration of all that diversity can bring to a company born of the digital age.

STARTING NEVER APART

One thing I learned from 10 years of running Lightspeed was that spaces are important. As a leader, you have to create a space, set an intention, fuel it, and fill it with your own energy and the energy of like-minded people. Then you have to listen, adapt, and allow it to unfold and grow. I would make the decision to turn 7049 St-Urbain into Never Apart, only knowing that it would have a spiritual intention to positively impact the world through culture, one cultural modality at a time.

I had not thought of Never Apart as an art gallery. I initially conceived of the space as a youth centre that could give back—the way that LGBTQ centres helped me and my friends growing up. Never Apart developed into a cultural program involving exhibitions, film screenings, music events, artist discussions, meditations, and other cultural and social happenings. And now, with three years under our belt, it has become clear that the intention of its original manifesto has guided the organic and radiant unfolding of the Centre, both within and beyond its walls.

While Never Apart was a project intended to connect *everyone* under the message of breaking down separations, I felt a deep commitment as a gay man to my own community. The name Never Apart, in fact, had a double meaning. It meant ending the separations that were at the heart of the challenges that humanity faced —between one another, between us and nature, and between us and our spiritual source. It was also a vow to LGBTQ people that never again would we be separated by others from our spiritual purpose in society.

Before we began the struggle for our civil rights and came forward as a community, we were the pioneers, the healers, the storytellers, the artists, the innovators, the radicals, the shamans, the caregivers, the messengers. With a gift for empathy, we were the unique few placed across all peoples and cultures to push society forward and defend its well-being. We offered divergent perspectives and brought people together in times of both joy and hardship. Our difference prepared us for this special calling.

We must remember that this was once our role, and that now, more than ever, the world needs us to step up to support the positive change and unity that are needed.

After three years of watching Never Apart reveal itself and explore so many aspects of the human spirit and identity through cultural means, the small seed of its manifesto finds itself re-examined and re-imagined in this book. That vision has been enriched by my personal learnings from both Never Apart and Lightspeed, my exchanges with the people who touched and influenced both projects, and my spiritual explorations along this journey.

Now is the time for an Age of Union, a vision for _unseparation_ in a fractured world. A call for changemakers to find purpose in action, to find intention in union, and be never apart.

Age of Union

Age of Union

In order to actualize our vision for a better world, it is worthwhile to zoom out and recontextualize our understanding of where humanity comes from, where our intentions lie today, and how we are already shaping our future. In short, we came from being in union with nature and in equilibrium with other species. We were once a part of nature's garden.

The history of *Homo sapiens* has been a blinding arc of progress. Our intelligence has allowed us to survive as a naked, vulnerable hominid, and then thrive and grow dominant on this planet in only a few thousand years—a relative blip in the four-billion-year history of our earth. During this time, we have applied our intelligence to create our own human systems, writing the unique narrative of humanity and transforming the planet to serve our own purposes.

THE ANTHROPOCENE

Yet the progress of humankind has been mirrored by social, environmental, and political calamities. All of our potential and progress has been tested in cycles of growth, war, and regression. On the one hand, our progress has yielded the most success, such as our efforts to fight global disease and infant mortality, and we have seen human lifespans and standards of living raised higher and faster than ever before. On the other, we have seen the human population and our level of consumption grow exponentially, and this has created catastrophic-scale stress on a planet with finite resources.

Our current geological epoch, the Holocene, dates back to the last ice age. For the past 12,000 years, the earth has had a relatively stable climate that has enabled humanity to flourish. During this time we were able to accelerate the development of our agricultural systems, which has culminated in the industrial, techno-logical, and biochemical advancements of the past 150 years. All throughout, we've crafted an *extractive* economy, fuelled by bound-less capitalism, against the grain of nature's circular systems in which species thrive and regenerate as a result of their interconnectedness.

Our economy of extraction has left permanent scars on eco-systems all over the world, from the deforested Amazon to the thinning sea ice of the Arctic. We've pushed extinction rates to a critical point, and we should prepare to see 50 per cent of our planet's biodiversity disappear from the earth by the end of this century. And not only that—we've introduced invasive species that disrupt the delicate balance of living ecosystems around the world. We've disturbed the ocean's circulation patterns and formed an entire new continent's worth of inorganic waste and plastic. We've dispersed radioactive elements across the globe. We are currently releasing carbon emis-sions into the atmosphere at the fastest rate since the extinction of the dinosaurs 66 million years ago,[3] and in doing so, we're unlock-ing permafrost from the thawing Arctic ice that contains more than twice the level of carbon than that in our air at present.

Scientists compellingly agree that we have actually entered a *new* geological epoch in which humans are the primary cause of deep and irremediable alterations to our physical landscape and biodiversity at large: the Anthropocene. This uncharted territory in human history is, according to scientists from the U.S. National Council, leading us toward the sixth major mass extinction in earth's history, whose scale will go beyond the impact we have had on our natural world and climate thus far. With the degree of species loss that is set to occur before we reach the year 2100, this is the future that we *already* inhabit.

Nature, however, is resilient. If we do succeed in destroying everything, life on earth will regenerate in 100 million years without humanity. The current Anthropocene is predated by five mass extinctions,[4] each of which saw, on average, 75 per cent of the planet's species disappear. The outlier is the End Permian (251 million years ago), known to paleontologists as "the Great Dying," an extinction where up to 96 per cent of all life on earth was annihilated. All of these mass extinctions had one thing in common: rapid climate change and a greenhouse effect caused by excess carbon dioxide in the atmosphere. Today, fossil fuels and other human activities are responsible for 10 billion tons of carbon released annually— 10 times more than at the start of the Late Paleocene Thermal Maximum, when global average temperatures reached more than 8 °C warmer than they are today.[5]

[3] World Meteorological Organization, *Statement on the status of the global climate in 2015* (Geneva: WMO, 2016).

[4] The End Ordovician (450–440 million years ago, 70% of species lost); the Late Devonian (375–360 million years ago, 70% of species lost); the End Permian (252 million years ago, 96% of species lost); the End Triassic (203 million years ago, 75% of species lost); and the End Cretaceous (66 million years ago, 75% of all species lost). Source: David M. Raup and J. John Sepkoski Jr., "Mass Extinctions in the Marine Fossil Record," *Science*, March 19, 1982, 1501–1503.

[5] World Meteorological Organization, *Statement on the status of the global climate in 2015* (Geneva: WMO, 2016).

Our changing climate and rising temperatures are already causing more human violence in our world, including an increase in violent crime and armed conflict.[6] Some researchers have proven that with every half-degree of warming, we typically see a 10 to 20 per cent increase in social and armed conflicts across the world. This can be explained by the scarcity of food due to extreme drought in densely populated regions (in Syria and Iraq, for example) as well as forced migrations and displacements caused by wildfires, floods, and extreme weather events.[7]

And while we fight one another without common direction for the future, the most urgent causes remain ignored. As a result, our ability to reverse the devastation induced by our ignorance diminishes year by year.

THE GREATEST LIGHT

Although living standards have been raised, we must acknowledge the damages that our thriving social and economic systems have caused: the liquidation and degradation of nature due to overpopulation and overconsumption, the growing gap between the rich and poor due to the concentration of wealth and resources among a select few, and a technologically driven globalization whereby the internet and automation are driving us toward an uncertain future with a lack of clear intention. This is the unsettling backdrop for what is, on a personal level for many, a time of feeling *lost*. There are too few people, places, and ideas from which to draw hope; there are too few to voice the belief that a direction exists that is not merely better for *some*.

Distrust in the system runs deep. For generations, people have been losing faith in political, economic, and religious institutions, and in the promise of technology, to create a better, more equitable, and sustainable future. These systems are driven by their own self-preservation and self-interest. They strengthen prevailing attitudes on how the world works, how we must behave, what rights we are granted, and where we are headed.

And yet, our greatest moments of uncertainty and fragmentation always precede our greatest revelations. Our darkest moment, in which we stand on the edge of social and ecological crisis, contains the seed of humanity's greatest opportunity —the seed of our greatest light.

We must believe that humanity is destined to do better. We must believe that a species of such high intelligence, ability, and promise can accept and act in its own long-term interests and care enough about our cradle of life to become its guardian.

SEEDS OF UNION

As we reach maturity as a species and gain understanding of the consequences of our dominant position on this earth, we must shift our worldview to reach a more conscious evolution of ourselves for the good of the planet.

We are here to protect creation in all its forms, and in that journey to connectedness we will fulfill our promise as a species: by reconciling the best of what we are with the beauty of what exists here in nature, by engaging with the culture of life, and by interlocking with its source. An Age of Union will be a celebration of creation. Every action we take can be infused with meaning and purpose. Every daily act can be an act of elevation. When our minds, hearts, and hands work toward this intention, we move beyond hope and into realization.

There are clear signs that we are ready. The tools exist for us to become globally aware and to act in unison. In spite of growing pains, the internet and social media allow us to spread awareness broadly. Creative entrepreneurs, innovators, and artists

---

[6] Courtney Plante, Johnie J. Allen, and Craig A. Anderson, "Effects of Rapid Climate Change on Violence and Conflict," *Oxford Research Encyclopedia of Climate Science* (April 2017).

[7] David Wallace-Wells, "The Uninhabitable Earth," *New Yorker*, July 9, 2017.

call us to action. We hunger for a modern sense of spirituality. We have the will to save the natural world and recognize the right of other species to thrive. We are ready to start.

Our next evolution has been called many things by many traditions; its existence is inevitable, but its contours have yet to be shaped. The "world to come" has been forming in our collective unconscious. It is the product of all of the difficult lessons, successes, and spiritual searches in human history. It has instilled in us an overwhelming need for profound change. An Age of Union is within our grasp. An Age of Union is possible now.

This book presents a vision of what an **Age of Union** can look like—a vision for how we can move beyond our separations—using culture, spirituality, and a reverence for nature as personal guides to ignite the leader within us. These are our **Pillars of Unseparation**.

Union is a powerful word. It speaks to our yearning to unify our inner separations between body and soul, and between thought, speech, and action. It appeals to our desire to connect our external separations, between cultures and identities, humanity and wilderness, consumption and the environment. This new culture of *unseparation* comes to life through **Acts of Union**, where union reveals itself in the intention we put toward our relationships, conversations, and actions.

This book is a guide to igniting the changemaker that exists in all of us, an invitation to add spark to the fire of a movement for positive change—to give rise to an age in which all living beings will be, once and for all, *never apart*.

Creating a better world does not happen overnight. We plant seeds today that can bring the beginnings of change in our generation and grow to bear fruit in future generations. One cannot see the full beauty of a tree in its seed. We understand that it will reach its fullness in time, and that the seeds that we nurture will bring the coming bounty.

The alternative is to continue on our current path—that of human division, species extinction on a mass scale, and environmental degradation. Humanity can do better.

It begins by examining the intentions behind each daily action. We must move toward recognizing the oneness across our world's exceptional diversity and begin to think beyond our individual selves, setting our intentions for the greater good.

These seeds of intention flower into thought, speech, and actions that lead to widening circles of change and transformation—to repair, correct, and unify the world—igniting our every act with meaning and purpose, glowing with the oneness, fullness, and understanding of union.

"If a person grasps a 'part' of unity he grasps
the whole, and the opposite is also true."
— Rabbi Israel Baal Shem Tov, *Keter Shem Tov.*

I woke from a dream in the middle of the night. Elephants were gathering to die in front of a house in an Indian village. In their eyes, I saw anguish and pain. I saw, and was filled with the depth of their loss. The elephants looked to humanity for the help they needed. They looked to us, hollow and beaten.

Earlier that week, there had been a story of human-animal conflict. In an area of India where refugees from civil war were encroaching on traditional elephant territories, a jeering mob of villagers set fire to an endangered Asian elephant and her calf.

Days later, the American president lifted the ban on big game trophy hunting, licensing the extinction of these intelligent, gentle, critically threatened creatures.

The days of being a spectator are over.

Age of Union

Pillars of Unseparation

To reveal the path toward *unseparation*, we must look to four pillars of hope and strength for humanity. These pillars will come to be understood in union: leadership, culture, spirituality, and nature.

Why these pillars? **Leadership** unlocks the potential for individuals to be agents of change in ways both large and small. **Culture** allows us to harness the potential of our identity, diversity, and expression to unify and share awareness among people. **Spirituality** supplies us with understanding of the oneness of all things and supplies the faith and strength to act for transformation. **Nature** helps us to think beyond the familiarity of our human experience on this planet and to value and protect that which is wild and unknown. A renewed love of nature, the guidance of spirituality, the strength and diversity of culture, and the confidence of a leader, when combined, can ignite transformative change, resilient union, and reveal our promise on this planet.

After exploring the four pillars and the culture of Never Apart, we will have an understanding of the intention of *unseparation* that lies in each of them. From there, intention must become action, and so the actions of change will be laid out in a final section—Acts of Union—which will help infuse our everyday thoughts, conversations, and actions with meaning and purpose, bringing us, act by act, into an Age of Union.

Age of Union

Leadership

The potential for everyone to see themselves as unique leaders or people of influence lights the path to an Age of Union and a better world.

Only creativity and a multiplicity of unique approaches can offer responsible pathways for humankind. Therefore, we need to harness and nurture a sense of leadership in individuals, at every stage of life's journey, in order to help build and usher in an Age of Union.

True leaders create leaders. Being impactful does not have to mean amplifying one's own voice above a great many—in our daily actions and conversations, in our exploration of paths toward change, and in our encouragement of others, we must find ways to nurture the leadership of others and become drivers of change.

Leadership is the first of the four pillars of *unseparation*.

Age of Union

POWER OF THE INDIVIDUAL

Individualism has reached its apex in our society. Increasingly, our lives are being accelerated by social media, ubiquitous consumerism, and mass information. In return, we have become more self-focused—a modern condition crystallized by the ever-pervasive *selfie*.

This dramatic shift in cultural normalcy—where the primacy of the community and the benefits of the collective have eroded and become secondary to individual freedoms, selfish concerns, and ephemeral desires—is a phenomenon sociologist Zygmunt Bauman describes as the *"liquidisation* of life."[8] According to Bauman, in a world that is rapidly changing and unstable, we tend to rely less and less on organized institutions, such as government, church, and traditional social ties. Instead, to keep afloat, we focus our lives on defining, perfecting, and affirming our individual identities through the abstract systems of what we consume, forms of leisure, projects of personal development, and professional realizations.

The positive side to this shift is that individual empowerment and self-driven action is critical to change; having an elevated confidence in and understanding of oneself allows one to be an impactful leader. One may lead with intentions that are oriented toward bringing meaning and purpose through action and immediacy. Understanding one's place in the social fabric is essential to contributing to society's greater good.

The negative side is that these character traits often lead us in the opposite direction, and farther away from union. Self-centredness turns the focus of our actions and our sense of self-empowerment inward. We tend to use our abilities to enrich ourselves, our standing, and our circle, to the exclusion and detriment of others and all else.

But it is important to recognize that our individuality is a powerful gift. Each and every one of us has the potential to be a leader. We all have the ability to demonstrate leadership to create and catalyze change, in large and small ways. With our unique spark of ability comes free will. Yet we have the potential to generate much more than the satisfaction of our own egos and desires. How we use our freedom is key to reaching an Age of Union.

Individuals have been the source of great change in this world. It all starts with the power of individuals to articulate their passion and cause ripples, and then waves of change. Every person is unique and therefore has the potential to contribute something uniquely meaningful to this world.

For humankind to produce broad change, we have to start thinking beyond ourselves as individuals in a vacuum. It takes courage to start thinking, speaking, and acting as leaders for the transformation we want to bring forward. Whether we are changemaking entrepreneurs, artists, policy influencers, engineers, scientists, or leaders in our own circles, our individual ability to lead with determination and lift others up is key to the large systemic renewal that we seek.

Leadership comes in many forms. It springs organically from the diversity of communities and from the wealth of expertise, cultural background, age, drive, and character of the individuals that form them. It is expressed in the desire to collaborate on goals that are greater than our own selves—a selflessness that is often its own reward. We can draw from that desire to contribute to our communities at every stage of our life's journey.

LIFE'S JOURNEY

Every stage of life offers the potential for leadership and growth. Our individual role in creating and contributing to union grows in the context of our life's journey. Each stage of our individual journey provides knowledge that can help drive our collective human capacity to be leaders for change.

[8] Zygmunt Bauman, *Liquid Life* (Cambridge: Polity, 2005).

As a **child**, we experience and learn from the world around us, reminding others of the goodness and innocence of our humble beginnings. We are taught the importance of listening and sharing. We learn the significance of courage and humility. If so exposed, we cherish animals and connect instinctively with nature.

As the author Richard Louv[9] seeks to remind us, being able to play in nature as a child is incredibly formative because wild nature presents itself to us with all of its variables and "loose parts," which trigger creativity, disruptive ideas, risk taking, cooperation, and organic leadership. It's the institutionalized education- and employment-based tracks leading toward adulthood that eventually break down these fibres of creativity and wonderment, making it harder to re-adopt our pure and wild spirit as we move through life.

As a **young adult**, we begin to interact and experiment with the world. At this age, we explore to find our passions. During this age of self-discovery, our scope is limitless. The teenage years are a central time to nurture creative and innovative ideas, learn how to navigate the inner workings of the collective, and understand our impact on others. We begin to nourish our soul in these ways and examine our own maturity. It is an opportune time to begin our own inner exploration.

In our **twenties and thirties**, we build our own world. Whether through a career, relationships, marriage, or having children of our own, we build the capacity and resources to know ourselves and develop our abilities to their full potential, while finding ways to contribute to the world through our journey of building. This is the time when we challenge ourselves the most as we try to find purpose and make a personal impact, testing the ways in which we can be part of the change. During these years of development, faith is an element that can sustain and strengthen us as we persevere—an important outcome of investing in our own spiritual journey.

In our **forties**, the mystical tradition[10] conveys, we receive the gift of understanding—the ability to look at the world with the benefit of experience. It is here, and in the decades that follow, that we have the resources, knowledge, and influence to reach our full potential, not only as individuals and family units, but as agents of change. Here we act to do all in our power to repair and unify the world, to make things better, to mentor those looking for guidance, while remaining engaged in our path, wherever it may lead us.

Our **fifties and sixties** bring the full maturity of life, often with the desire to follow new paths. We benefit from this energy and wisdom to plant the next seeds of life. Love, work, and spirituality are looked upon differently. Here we enjoy the serenity of being who we truly are and having the confidence to do, in the world, what we believe is right, with the sagacity to inspire younger generations.

In our **senior years**, we become the elders of society. We contribute a great deal in terms of mentorship and guidance, influencing upcoming generations while doing all we can to bring about change and unity. We keep an eye toward the past, present, and future, reflecting on a life's journey devoted to personal growth, connecting, giving to others, and working actively for the guardianship of animals and nature—all for the love and aspiration of union.

While every person's path is different, it is important to understand that, like a tree, we begin as a seed. We find the air first as a sapling and grow over a lifetime into a member of the forest, bringing beauty, shelter, wisdom, and guardianship to life around us. We draw from the depth of our roots in the ground and transform energy from the sources above to bring strength and vitality into this world. One day we again become part of the soil, adding once more to its fertility, but not before we have spread the seeds of our influence and learning, passing on our spark to future generations.

[9] Richard Louv, *Last Child in the Woods: Saving Our Children From Nature-Deficit Disorder* (New York: Workman Publishing, 2005).

[10] In the Jewish mystical tradition, the gift of *binah*, or "understanding" in Hebrew, is given at the age of forty, representing the fullness of one's ability to apply one's life's experience.

DIVERSITY OF LEADERSHIP

There is a stereotype in our culture of what a leader must look like. Collectively, we need to broaden our narrow notions of leadership to embrace its many styles and faces. Difference is a great teacher. Fear difference, and you learn nothing. Leadership diversity means more creativity, ingenuity, and ability in our world —more inclusivity—to help us reach a unified age.

In this more encompassing definition of leadership, you may ask yourself, "Where do I fit in?" Leadership can be found in many areas of life. We often think of public, political, or business leaders, but leaders can also be found in the community, in the workplace, in our personal circles, and at home. Diverse leaders bring diverse contributions to the world:

A visionary leader mobilizes people toward an idea.

A coaching leader develops people for the future.

An affiliative leader creates emotional bonds and harmony.

A democratic leader builds consensus through participation.

A pacesetting leader sets an example of excellence and self-direction.

QUALITIES OF A LEADER

No matter the style of leadership, there are some qualities that every leader should work to incorporate into their practice and continue to improve upon. The first is **listening**. Great leadership is forged from the ability to understand a problem or scenario with as much input from as many perspectives as possible, apply the wisdom of personal experience, and operate on a basis of knowledge that combines both. Being an active listener with your colleagues, your employees, your stakeholders, and even with your family and friends will allow you to better conceive your vision and create profound solutions.

In the same spirit, it is also important for a leader to **create seats at the table** for different perspectives. Complete projects cannot be developed without diverse ideas—and being approachable and receptive as a leader to create space for others to be heard is essential to encourage such an exchange. No matter the objective, the act of listening invests others in moving forward with a final decision.

For a business or social leader, listening is also an important way to **share ownership** and drive people toward results-oriented outcomes. But distributing ownership is only possible when there is trust and accountability. Trust comes not from perfect behaviour but from accountability.[11] No one can be expected to be perfect, but a healthy person can be expected to be accountable, acknowledge an error, and own it. Trust means that your attitude and conduct over time demonstrate that you can be depended upon and that you have the integrity to act appropriately even when no one is watching.

Leaders cannot do it all on their own: **developing a community of allies** and building a team is key. Before one can inspire initiative or ownership, one must learn how to bring the right people into the fold. Leaders need to be able to set aside their ego and, where they lack experience and knowledge, to attract people with specialized knowledge into a project.

Leaders need to be able to **communicate and build energy** around their vision, presenting how the big picture can be attained through the contributions of all. Leaders should identify and reward integrity and trustworthiness, to educate, support, mentor, and grow individuals as they join a common cause.

[11] Simon Jacobson, *Toward a Meaningful Life, New Edition: The Wisdom of the Rebbe Menachem Mendel Schneerson* (self-published teachings of the Lubavitcher Rebbe, 2004), 99.

Making difficult decisions is one of the most challenging responsibilities of any leader. In seeing the broadest picture possible and by incorporating diverse voices into your process, you are able to make the call that best reflects the choice, or priority, that is wisest for your endeavour and that contributes to the greater goal of union. The right trade-offs and choices are sometimes obvious, but sometimes less so. Making the right decision often requires both wisdom and faith from a leader. Decision making also requires a willingness to fail and a readiness to find new solutions constructively.

A leader is **responsible for the work culture** of a project. Whether it's a physical space or an online forum, we must set the tone for a safe, diverse, inclusive, accepting, listening, and action-oriented culture. Leaders, by their example and by the ways in which they set the tone for exchange and action, will find their style mirrored and emulated, thus setting the culture so that others can amplify and multiply it.

A leader can multiply this elevation by **being a role model** and reference in how they lead and act. One only has to look at small business owners aiming to revitalize their neighbourhoods, engineers striving toward medical or clean energy breakthroughs, teachers educating generations of students on the history of civil rights, local leaders pledging to support the LGBTQ persons in their communities struggling to find their place, or conservationists fighting for the protection of wilderness, in order to see leadership working within the fine threads of our society. For Jane Goodall, Sylvia Earle, Martin Luther King Jr., Malala Yousafzai, Laxmi Narayan Tripathi, and Stephen Hawking, and for every single person who has dared to think differently and seek alternative paths toward a better future, the difficult moments have likely outnumbered the winning ones in their lives.

Becoming a thought leader in your industry or area of activity is a way to generate a conversation with others and share tools for success through open dialogue. Think beyond "what can you do for me?" and instead consider "how can we support each other?" Seek constant learning for yourself and others through dialogue with your peers. You should not only take part in this exchange, but try to lead the conversation. Getting involved with forums and conferences, for instance, promotes healthy, trusting relationships both within your project's community and among local, interconnected communities. At its roots, your intention should be selfless. Uplifting those around you should be part of the mandate and mission of your project.

OVERCOMING ECHO CHAMBERS

As leaders, we must also be curious about others and reach out for diverse viewpoints, which, in return, will make our ideas richer, our understanding deeper, and our opinions more nuanced. It is therefore important to reach out to those who operate and think differently from us across all cultures and age groups. But one may wonder how one can learn from or influence those who have diametrically opposite views. Our world is polarizing, and online platforms and social media have had the opposite effect of what many had hoped they might in terms of fostering global consciousness.

Algorithmic coding and its recent applications across social media and paid ad space are designed to emphasize *homophily* —a natural tendency to associate with people of the same age, background, and perspective. It also pronounces our propensity for tribalism, which, when taken to its extreme, limits our social diversity, creating dangerous echo chambers of opinion and belief.

As a result, online communications, which are disrupted by algorithms designed to sell more effective advertisements, become increasingly fragmented and lack depth, quality, and diversity. The more these communications are mutually reinforced, the more they will be infused with attributes of polarity and lead to disunity and violence.

The digital fragmentation of our communications means a fragmentation of our culture. This is therefore an opportunity for us to actively use modes of cultural expression and exchange to break down separation and bring about unity. We must be proactive and vigilant in finding ways to enlarge our circle, to create opportunities to know and listen to people who are not like us, and to search out and learn about animal species and ecosystems that we are unfamiliar with.

The more we know and understand, the more we will be able to connect and unify beyond the existing barriers that impede union. We should always be looking for tools that can elevate our humanity, empower a diversity of leaders, and celebrate the richness of our differences.

MULTIPLYING LEADERSHIP

Becoming an influential figure within a group of one's peers —family, friends, and community—is never easy, and never without obstacles. But following how we feel is worth our effort. Our sense of purpose can give people a positive purpose of their own.

Leadership is a chain reaction. Individuals who stand up for what is right can cause ripples of action in the people immediately around them. The internet amplifies this effect. While social platforms can trigger self-indulgence and divisiveness, they can also be an empowering tool for the Age's leaders to promote positive change and unity to a global audience. The internet is the single most powerful catalyzing force for union because it has democratized the modes of communication such that everyone can be an agent of change.

Change is required on many fronts, from individual and household to municipality, state, country, and planet. It requires people of all ages, of all ethnic backgrounds, of all genders, and of all identities to lead in big and small ways, to embrace their individual potential, and to work with others to advance awakening and transformation.

Great leaders naturally build more leaders. A true leader also knows when to follow another's lead, lending support when the latter's contribution to the world is having a positive impact. To achieve an Age of Union, leaders must value the ideas of people who are willing to change our social, economic, and political struc-tures—people who do not fit the current mold, who do not yet have a seat at the table. We must listen to them, we must support them, and we must create space for them to lead as well. Diverse and collective leadership will allow us to craft a world that reflects our deeper aspirations.

Individuals are capable of creating great change. The potential for everyone to see themselves as leaders or people of influence, in their own way, lights the path to a better world. If we band together across our diversity and lead with the intention of uplifting one another to seek union, the potential is enormous for us to effect positive change and transforma-tion that can bring us collectively into a new age.

LEADERSHIP AT LIGHTSPEED

I was fortunate to have been raised with a strong sense of self and individuality. From my cultural background to coming out in my early teens and forging my career path, to my cultural and spiritual inclinations, I have always identified as someone with a firm sense of who I was, but I have also stayed continually curious as to how I could explore beyond my boundaries. Spiritual growth has allowed me to do this in so many ways. It has freed me to explore in the knowledge that I am building and investing in myself in ways that may be of broader use later—not just to me, but hopefully to others as well.

It wasn't until I started my own company at age 28 that I began to see myself as a leader. In previous contracts or jobs, I had never led teams. For the first few years of Lightspeed, I was the lead developer, and so the value I was bringing to the fledgling project was clear. Programming until 4 a.m. for two straight years was certainly needed to build the company's product and foundation. But during the day, when I would walk down the back stairs of the two connected studio apartments (one my home and the other the office) to work on the business itself, I took note of how the team looked to me for guidance about our goals and how we would go about accomplishing them.

Later, as the company grew, I delegated many of my responsibilities to others on the team, including the programming tasks. Each reinvention of my role was at first uncomfortable, yet necessary in order for us to grow. This yearly reinvention of what is needed from me as a leader is critical to our scalability. It remains consistently important for me to distribute ownership among my team and instill leadership in them so that I can share the responsibility—celebrating their successes and our common achievements while also supporting them fully when faced with failure.

I would define my leadership style as empowering, optimistic, unifying, risk-taking, and supportive. As a member of the LGBTQ community, you may find yourself in a similar position as I was. I never saw myself as having the Type-A characteristics of traditional leaders. I chose instead to leverage my position by valorizing diverse perspectives. This has allowed me to find my own methods of leadership, elevated by the voices of others.

Without this foundation of trust in others, it is difficult to take the risks necessary to achieve breakthroughs. I have striven to enlist team members who share my values and with whom I can share ownership. I recognized early on that no project is scalable if you cannot place trust in your colleagues—and nothing of significance can ever be built if your colleagues' sense of ownership doesn't push them to achieve what you would in their place. Building up leadership in others and providing them with the cultural environment and tools to succeed opens up unlimited possibilities, allows people to do the best work of their lives, and brings all of their unique talents to the table.

Even when everyone makes their best effort, there will always be moments of failure. We experience failure every day, multiple times a day, in large and small ways. Failure is a part of making progress. Failure is learning. Those 10 cuts you endure in a day as a leader have to be absorbed as new understanding and calls to action, while the two successes become your fuel to push forward.

While our efforts and the wisdom of our decisions have a bearing on whether we succeed or fail, the truth is that there are limits to what we can control. We can put our best selves forward and have faith in our path, but we must also learn to let go. This is where having a spiritual foundation is important. Having faith in my vision was one thing. But having enough faith to fully let go of the burden I carried in order to draw from something greater was a process that allowed me to pass through my most challenging moments at Lightspeed.

This is an easy thing to forget. You begin to claim all of the successes, and you begin to internalize all of the failures. In my experience, it is best to let go of both, and recognize your leadership role as an instrument, a conduit, or a stewardship of something that is beyond you and your doing alone. When your intentions come from a place of greater contribution, you can gain the freedom and strength to align your project with your greater purpose.

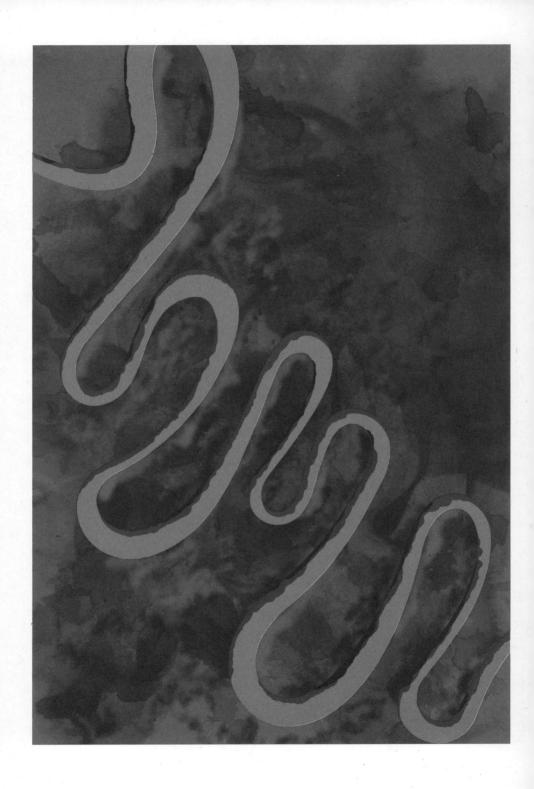

Age of Union

Culture

The richness of our world lives in culture. Politics, religion, and economics exert strong influences on culture through the creation of boundaries, whereas technology, creativity, and entrepreneurship allow us to cross those borders and unite in various ways. We have to begin from a place where we are collectively taking initiative to understand and value our diversity of identity and expression. Only then can we be enriched by the experiences of one another and stand together.

But first, why is culture so central to bringing about an Age of Union? We must discover union through diversity, new perspectives, and cultural innovations. We must contemplate and consider the positive effects of opening up dialogues of identity, learn from one another's creative transmissions, and allow these journeys to play out and commingle within our various cultural arenas. We all desire the freedom to be ourselves, be understood, be compassionate, be connected, and be *never apart*. To achieve this, we must allow others the same freedoms.

THE KEYS OF CULTURE

We are wired to see the world in dualities—a world of straight lines and opposites: men vs. women, gay vs. straight, city vs. nature, left vs. right, art vs. science, and so on. As a result, we're wired to define our individuality within these binary systems. It is a very human instinct to compartmentalize and try to make logical that which is beyond our understanding.

As we have advanced through civilizations, we have seen separations grow: continents divided into countries, countries into states and regions; people splintered across tribes, villages, towns, cities; neighbourhoods split across ethnic origins, economic strata, and religious backgrounds. We have widened our separation from nature and from other species. The smaller the pieces that we have been broken down into, the easier it has been for groups to gain power and dominion over the parts.

This current social and political climate exploits differences between people to divide us—hence the idiom "divide and conquer." Tribalism and demagoguery frame the world in terms of zero-sum binaries. Polarization creates culture wars where there must always be a winner and a loser. In this worldview, diversity is not understood as a resource for solutions. Rather, the idea of diversity is used to stoke the fear of otherness and manufacture xenophobia by those who benefit from segregating people who are simply looking for answers.

However, the culture, or collective narrative, of the "tribe" of humanity often places greater value on some parts of the whole than on the whole itself. We seek to label, conclude, and control the pieces, rather than embrace our share in the greater whole. Individually, we experience the outcomes of this separation; we continually struggle with being pulled apart, and once we are *woke* to this reality, we resist it. As a result, our cultural differences impose further separation.

Cultural differences are still not fully considered sources of strength and beauty, even though the world proves to us, again and again, how connected we are. Through our shared humanity, through culture, and within a balanced natural ecosystem, we thrive both in diversity and union.

The language of this cultural unity is understanding. The alternative to division and tribalism is what we have come to call *unseparation*, and that requires us to see differences for what they truly are: expressions of humanity that bear the knowledge of different paths of ancestry, belief, and life experience, as well as of different approaches. Our curiosity about these *othernesses* has the power to dispel fear and ignorance. Therefore culture, when seen in the full splendour of its variety, can be a unifying force. When we all come to the table with openness and a willingness to share and to receive, we begin to understand, empathize, and unite across the chasm.

As an example of the powerful value of diversity, inclusion, and cultural expression, the progress of the LGBTQ rights movement showcases how bringing people in from the margins and celebrating cultural mixing can uplift and elevate all of society. Since the LGBTQ community "came out" during the 1969 Stonewall Riots in New York City, it and its members have been able to slowly reconcile the otherness of their life experiences with their integration into society. This has resulted in their social progress, such as the legal recognition of their relationships in marriage and of their worldview and cultural contribution to our society. At the same time, the world experiences the value of diversity as it seeks to understand its power.

CULTURE AS IDENTITY

The first way to understand our own arena of culture is in the many ethnic, political, religious, and economic groups to which we may simultaneously belong as individuals. These exert strong cultural influences on our behaviour and outlook. Our social circles —friends, family, personal and professional communities—also shape how we see the world. Gender identity and sexuality introduce layers of culture to this colourful collection of attributes that help us build our sense of self.

All of these cultural networks create bonds between people, allowing us to be a part of groups that share common values, beliefs, and experiences. As we enter a new globalized era, we may each belong to multiple cultural circles, and we may find ourselves to be the cultural product of many different, often disparate and conflicting, influences. The growing complexity of our individual identities makes us adaptable, and more understanding and empathetic toward others.

The strength of diversity shines where we lack understanding and answers. Seeking input and knowledge from people's diverse backgrounds will lead to finding richer solutions to the world's problems, solutions that work for all and not just a select few.

As cosmopolitan cities grow, the internet expands, and easier access to travel is made available, we are given further opportunities to build greater connections with people who are different from us at first glance. We can bond and bind new social tribes together with those that are inherently different from us but with whom we share a common spark. We can enjoy the discovery of commonality, but also enrich ourselves by learning from our differences.

CULTURE AS EXPRESSION

The second means to understanding culture is through the lens of creative expression and our collective and personal experiences of it. Art, music, food, film, photography, dance, performance, literature, and architecture are all modes of cultural expression that can showcase one's heritage, beliefs, and influences. They can offer new ways of looking at something, broadening our worldview and opening our minds.

Creative and artistic expression connects people on deeper levels of consciousness. It cuts across the differences of our daily lived realities and speaks to our soul—a depth of our humanity where we share much more with each other than we realize. Since we experience creativity and artistic work within our daily lives (visiting an exhibit, watching a film, listening to new music, etc.), the presence of cultural forms of expression shows us that our lives are radiantly multi-hued and joyously unpredictable. Yet it also shows us that this life and this world are multi-dimensional. Culture in the former sense often stops at the edges of borders or at the edges of a family lineage, but culture in the latter sense cuts across all geographical spaces and times to reveal a world that is boundless, timeless, and infinitely connected. Culture is a weapon against homogeneity, against oppression, against submission, and against isolation.

For these reasons, it's imperative that we embrace and support cultural expression in all its forms and attempt in our own ways to make culture a part of our daily lives.

Every creative act has the potential to communicate one's inner thoughts and desires, give voice to the marginalized, stimulate one's senses, build new worlds, heal emotional fractures, and promote empowerment. But most importantly, "making" connects us—with nature, with one another, with our ancestors, and with the spiritual pulse that beats within us.

Our creative endeavours have infused humankind with communicative bridges since the beginning of our era. Yet it is only with the digital age and our access to design tools, instantaneous publishing platforms, and social networks that we have been able to create and share within borderless global communities. Even if today's internet features heightened behavioural imbalances, polarizing communication algorithms, addictive feedback loops, and rights-infringing surveillance and tracking, it has allowed us to move beyond the age of sitting back and being told what to think and toward an *unseparated* age of dialogue and collaboration.

"Creative cultural expression carries with it the potential for us all to become agents of great change in the world."
— David Gauntlett, author of *Making Is Connecting*

Every creative act has
the power to connect us.

THE CULTURAL PURPOSE OF TECHNOLOGY

Technology has had a massive impact on humanity and the trajectory of culture. Technology is an ever-forward-moving force shaping our identity. It is how we express ourselves, how we work, and how we interact with the world. We have held up an ideal that technology will bring solutions to our growing separations, and we are not wrong. There is an incipient potential to bring about greater union and collective consciousness through technology. But today's reality reveals that we must also add human judgement and wisdom, and if possible emotion and ethics, to the applications of tech.

We have seen positive and negative outcomes in recent iterations of online dialogue and the growing influence of automation and big data. Never before has the world been so connected and aware of our social and environmental problems. But we are also kept separated into target markets for advertisers and political interest groups. Data, automation, and AI are biased toward those who control the technology. Is "big tech" becoming "Big brother"? In a world where we are witnessing growing inequality and where we feel unanchored in the wake of rapid change, we must pause to relearn our own humanity. We must adapt technology to our needs and make it our instrument to create positive social and environmental change.

From ancient times, humans have tried to predict the future, whether through astrological systems or agricultural almanacs. Data generated from sources all around us and from our own interactions and personal information will allow AI systems to make predictions and create new levels of efficiency and optimization in a newly unfolding reality. Will this mean further inequality between those who control the data and the power of prediction, and those who don't —the "data rich" vs. the "data poor"? Will opportunities continue to be made available to us all as automation and AI further disrupt past industrial models?

These are big questions that we will have to answer in our societies as AI advances and the world becomes more deeply reliant on predictive models and their inherent biases. We will need to more deeply understand and internalize what makes us uniquely human and how we will apply ethics to AI-based decision making where there is less and less human consideration and intervention. We must create technology that is designed to make us better humans and that can mirror our deeper aspirations.

Creating the Never Apart non-profit after 10 years of running Lightspeed revealed to me how much may be learned from the culture of innovation that forms the DNA of a tech startup. Projects across a broad spectrum can benefit from the ideas and frameworks that help startups foster creativity and leverage technology to enable new ways of achieving goals and inventing new approaches to problems.

Leveraging technology to build new lines of communication and adopting new tools can be multipliers of effort and allow better solutions to be created by having forums for ideas and distilling perspectives into new answers and approaches. The instinct of a tech startup is to be in a constant state of reinvention and self-disruption to keep our thinking adaptive and agile.

We are in the early stages of being globally connected through the internet. This new path toward being globally conscious of our strengths and challenges cannot have come sooner given what we are facing collectively with existential environmental crises such as climate change and mass extinction. Problems across societies and between states exist today as they have throughout the history of humanity. However, today's human-caused planetary condition is showing rapid decline and this is the most urgent issue we must all face together.

Yet in these early stages of the internet, in the midst of these teething lessons of social media, we have seen a focus on the self and distraction rather than on developing the tools for creating critical mass in support of positive global change. We have seen early applications of AI prediction and big data that benefit marketers more than citizens, species, and ecosystems. We must reclaim these advances of technology to uplift one another as leaders for change, to create awareness of our challenges, and to gain understanding of those outside our echo chambers.

Most of all, we cannot forget to live outside our screens. We must reconnect to one another, and to nature, our great teacher. Technology can facilitate this and, if used with intention and purpose, its use can be guided from the soul to bring about an Age of Union.

"Art is the silent activist."
— Ekaterina Sky

CULTURE AS CHANGE AGENT

Cultural expression builds bridges between peoples, creates conversations where there was once silence, and reveals the patterns of our identities. Music, which Rabbi Schneur Zalman of Liadi famously called "the pen of the soul," is often said to be a universal language with the power to combine and connect our songs of spirit with one another.

For the audience of a creative work, a new world of understanding is introduced. Whether one's intent is to provide social commentary, provoke thought, raise awareness and educate, communicate a mood, or express a new idea, our reception of a work of art can take many forms. We may be allowed to feel a connection to the artists themselves or to their perspectives, to feel moved by a work alone, to internalize and intellectualize the message privately, or to reflect on our own context and perspective. Art allows us all this freedom. In this way, art is more than a one-way expression. It is a distinctly human way to connect the experiences of people coming from different places and perspectives, binding them for a moment in a confluence of culture, and affecting emotionally all who are present in this moment.

All forms of creative cultural expression can bring people together, breaking through to create a shared awareness that frees us from the bonds of preconception that are designed to keep us divided. In this way, our modes of culture become active agents of transformation and a powerful voice for union.

BUILDING A CULTURE OF DIVERSITY

Culture is a unifying force because it builds understanding where there is disconnection and fear. War, racism, and sexism are divisions that have been destructive forces in our history—a tragic waste of lives, energy, and resources that keeps us from building the world in which we want to live.

Now is our opportunity to deprogram the cultural constructs inherited from previous, less tolerant, and less globally conscious eras and rebuild society's great bridges with knowledge, empathy, and understanding.

Just as nature itself thrives off a diverse ecosystem, the world is rich with many different kinds of people, cultures, and communities with diverse religious, spiritual, literary, artistic, culinary, and social backgrounds. To become a truly peaceful and inclusive society, we must open our circles, create seats at the table, and allow diverse perspectives to be heard and incorporated into solutions. Concretely, this takes effort because deviating from our regular approaches forces us out of the comfort zone of our process, and uncertainty can be difficult to embrace. Yet advancement does not come without effort and readjustment—*unseparation* takes work.

It is by considering our daily actions with the intent to look beyond ourselves, and by enriching our culture and world with the light of diversity, that we will achieve the ideals of an Age of Union.

A vibrant, resilient forest finds its strength in variation. A tree plantation with only one kind of tree will not survive a forest fire or a plague due to a lack of diversity. Humanity is poorer when it limits itself to only one perspective, to thinking as a monoculture or tribe.

FINDING OUR PURPOSE AS LGBTQ PEOPLE

LGBTQ people are part of the oneness of creation. We have all the potential to teach the value of diversity through the fusion of our own culture. From the beginnings of humanity we have served a spiritual purpose, distributed by design across all societies as philosophers, artists, writers, designers, caregivers, healers, storytellers, leaders, and messengers. Standing simultaneously inside and outside society, we have straddled the dual roles of being both passive observers and active contributors.

In the last 50 years, we have emerged as a community and gradually gained the right to live as we are. After fighting for our rights, beginning with Stonewall, we came out as a defined community in the 1970s. We lived a form of absolute freedom and discovery in the 1970s and 1980s and we began our fight for our civil rights to be recognized. But almost immediately, our populations and our morale were slashed, clear-cut like a forest, by the health crisis of the HIV/AIDS plague. We persevered and kept working for our freedoms, and in the last few years we have managed to win the right to be married and love freely in many Western countries. No other group in history has been able to acquire civil rights so rapidly. It shows how powerfully integrated LGBTQ people are within society, even though in many places universal acceptance is still an uphill battle.

We still don't have access to the benefits of full equality. People are still hostile toward what they don't understand. Fighting for our civil rights and our universal acceptance is an ongoing struggle. But as important as this is to our community, we cannot fight for our pride and our right to exist without understanding our greater purpose. We must understand and embrace the intention of our design. In the absence of a direction and a spiritual context, many in our community are challenged by feelings of being lost and unanchored. Some cope with this through self-centred behaviour, isolation, or addiction. But we have to realize that our existence is a gift and that our lives can guide and inspire others—those who also feel lost and unanchored. Because we exist outside the norms of society, our place naturally questions the very fabric of society's constructs, and its formulas and patterns.

And now, in the age of technology, when all is connected, we are called to our greatest purpose yet. Never before have we been needed so urgently as leaders of this changing world. An Age of Union requires messengers. It requires hope. It requires hearts and minds be transformed, humanity to be harmonized with creation, and action be taken to bring peace between diverse peoples.

We can do all this. We can take the lead. That which is least understood, that which is cloaked in the deepest mystery, will bring the brightest light.

LGBTQ people are an unrevealed spark, ready to bridge dualities and reveal the spectra of identity in ways that could only have been gifted by the source. We are a testament to the power, beauty, and spiritual design of the diversity of creation. Our undeniably unique gifts and our distribution among all people are how we are designed to contribute to this world. We are great communicators and great connectors. We can be the source of connection in society and culture, and we can be great lights. Even those who have the least, or who are the most fractured and scarred in our community, bring joy and beauty to other people, because that is our second nature. Our gifts will have their revelation; they will be drawn out in order to draw down the spiritual and help bring about an Age of Union.

We will be examples. We will show the best of humanity's potential. We will prove the value and strength of diversity. We will protect the natural world. We will light humanity's path with pride and purpose.

Age of Union

Spirituality

All great movements for change in human history have been powered by belief and purpose. The belief in something greater than ourselves has given humanity the perspective to think beyond our own individual needs and commit our minds, hearts, and hands to the greater good. As such, we feel a spiritual reward when we bring good into the world.

However, in today's modernized world, we have lost a sense of meaning and purpose in our actions. We are taught that we are independent and self-reliant, the sole source of what we create. Our lives are too often driven by our own gain. As we become more connected through technology, we become less connected to the traditions and gatherings of our communities. As we become more secular and rational, we diminish our understanding that spirituality, or even nature, is bigger than ourselves. We have become used to bending everything to our individualism, turning all to our will and desire.

Age of Union

BODY, SOUL, AND SPIRIT

Spirituality is the journey of connecting into something larger than our own existence. It allows individuals to grow on a personal level by giving and serving the greater good. It also allows us to nourish our own soul—our connection to a greater purpose.

While we understand the body and its physical wants, many of us don't fully understand how to fulfill the needs of the soul. We may not fully understand that this is the part of us that belongs to something greater than ourselves, connected to a universal, unified source in a transcendent way that our body, with its physical constraints, is not. When we begin to look inward, we discover that our soul is connected to a source from which great strength can be drawn. We must make this connection to bring about the tremendous transformations we seek.

Mysticism tries to explain that which lies beyond the limits of science. It can be understood as the ancient human interpretation of something beyond our comprehension—of the divine, if you will. That said, it remains a personal choice to seek its guidance in interpreting experiences that can't be quantified by science. As one of the paths that I have chosen to explore on my own journey, I present mystical thought to you for your consideration, stating unequivocally that it is one of many, and not the only path to spiritual exploration.

What, then, does mysticism tell us about the body, soul, and spirit? Our body and soul both come from the same source. All things are united in oneness, from the inanimate mountains, rivers, and rocks to the living plants, animals, and people. All is connected and infused with the infinite creative source—a source that is one with creation itself.

The body is material and the soul is spiritual. In the mystical tradition, the body was created first, from dust, and the soul was created second, from the breath that filled our body and brought it to life. The breath, which can be regarded as either wind or spirit, connects us to the divine. The body is our instrument. It has its own physical needs and wants. Without the influence of the soul, its role is to preserve the self and it is therefore vulnerable to our own desires and ego. United with the soul, however, the body can be used to bring our spiritual awareness into the physical realm. When we do not nourish the soul, it is a flame burned down to its embers. It will never be extinguished, but it will languish as our body's physical demands and natural desires dominate our thought, speech, and action.

When nourished, the soul is a flame. It burns brightly, lighting our path through the world. Our flame grows into a fire. It fuels our human promise and radiates outwards, lighting the world that surrounds us. When we ignite the flames of others, our own is not depleted. No matter how many wicks draw light from the source, it cannot be diminished. We are all connected through the light of the source. When we look past the physical, past material separations, we realize that, collectively, we can add to the growing light of union.

UNION BEGINS WITHIN

One of the first steps in renewing our world is having a better understanding of our soul. This spiritual knowing renews our intentions, thought, speech, and action. If the intention of our souls were to align in an Age of Union, collectively we could bring about great change. There are many mystical lenses and many spiritual paths to guide our alignment. However, common to each is the truth that union begins within.

Before we can connect with one another, before we can connect with animals and nature, before we can connect with our spiritual source, we must reach inward to find that which connects our body and our soul. When we open our hearts to spirituality, when we allow the soul to lead us toward union, we receive an outpouring of meaning and purpose—inspiration out of the breath of creation.

What concrete benefit might result from learning to understand the pairing of the body and the soul? How might this union actually manifest itself as a positive change in our daily lives?

Think of an intention as a seed that contains all of its own potential. The seed remains intact while it awaits a catalyst to bring it to life. Depending on how we care for the seed in our thoughts, we may one day witness this good intention bear fruit and thrive.

The seed of intention germinates into thoughts. How we fill our thoughts greatly influences outcomes in our lives and our experience on our planet. If we dwell with a pure intention, positive thoughts can lead us to build bridges and break down the separations that hold the world back.

However, if we dwell in negative attitudes, we must ask ourselves where these attitudes come from and where they will take us. As our intention germinates, we must ask ourselves where the speech and actions derived from these negative attitudes might lead us, and we must seek to realign our thoughts.

Speech, either spoken or written, is our unique way of bringing ideas into the world. According to mystical thought, human speech mirrors the divine sounds, vibrations, and utterances that were made when the world was formed during creation.

When we speak, we choose our words carefully, constraining our thoughts in order to externalize them. Speech is thus at once revealing and concealing. We say one thing while we conceal another. We refine our thoughts in order to share them. We speak to make space for something new. In this way, speech is an act of creation that is akin to the origins of creation itself. The infinite source, by constricting itself, made space for creation, formed the universe, and gave shape to all that would follow.

The act of speech brings us to the final step in an intention's journey: taking action. An action whose origins are aligned with an intent to create union will generate an array of positive impacts. Concrete action may resonate with and positively affect another's intention. Thus, a single action can multiply and contribute to generating broad transformation.

The true goal of developing our sense of spirituality is to bring concrete, positive action into the world by establishing our own inner union. Having inner union and inner peace are great aspirations, but having inner union that translates intention into action is a powerful way to think about the actual outcomes of our spiritual journey. In positively intended action, we see that the union of the body and soul has transformed an intention into positive actions in the physical world.

The mystics tell us that our purpose is to repair the world in this lifetime, preparing the way and creating a home for divinity in our physical world. Our thought, speech, and action must therefore be rooted in the now, anchored in our daily choices.

If we consider the alternative, we don't have to look far to find examples of actions around the world that indicate the absence of the soul. Actions taken with no regard for the greater good, without empathy, or without any compassion for others illustrate the consequences of being guided only by the self, by want, and by desire. Here we see the worst of the human instinct result in actions that benefit only the self and fuel greed, division, ignorance, and destruction.

This is why the union of body and soul must guide us on all levels in an Age of Union.

When humanity first discovered fire, we also discovered its promise and its danger. Fire brought us unlimited warmth, light, and protection, and yet it also gave us the power to destroy. Fire is a symbol of both the best and the worst of humanity's power.

In modern times, fire represents the promise of embracing the power of the sun. For example, nuclear fusion and solar could provide us with clean, everlasting energy. Fire symbolizes the light we could bring into the world. But the fires of war and industry also bring environmental degradation, suffering, and destruction.

We must master the fire and ignite the human spirit to bring about an Age of Union. Let the human flame become a symbol of the wisdom of our power. Let our flame rise up to the source, grow, and add light.

THE SOUL

My understanding of the soul is mapped by the mystical tradition. Of the soul's five levels, the nearest level is very much attached to the body, as though the soul had an anchor in the body that rises up like a flame, yearning for its source. The soul is therefore rooted in the physical, but has ascending levels that rise up until it reaches the final level—total unity with the source.

During one of my trips to Israel, I learned why it is a common and ancient practice to visit graveyards. It is believed that the most physical part of the soul remains attached to the body even after death and burial. So, there is a part of the soul that can still be visited at a gravesite. By connecting with this physical part of the soul of an ancestor, we can therefore join with the parts of the soul that are no longer constrained by the boundaries of the body, the soul's vessel.

Many of us in our everyday lives operate only at a very basic spiritual level and focus mostly on meeting our immediate physical needs. When you aspire to be more spiritually connected, you can start climbing the ladder of your own soul and connecting with its higher levels, reaching toward the source.

At the base of existence is the world of action, the physical world. As we ascend the levels of the soul, we climb to the worlds of formation, creation, and emanation—ever closer to the source. If we look at this from the top down, spiritual light cascades from the world of emanation to the world of action.

Mysticism helps us visualize that the soul is designed in a very similar way: it starts with *emanation* at the top. Emanation is will and intention. There is always a seed of intention that then cascades from nothingness to the creation of thought, to the formation of speech and action. From the soul at its highest level, the purely spiritual cascades all the way down to the physical.

When we do something in the physical world with intention, we elevate this act beyond the physical to the spiritual. If we act with a spiritual purpose, a spiritual intent and awareness, then we elevate the act. We elevate the world. You climb that ladder through the everyday actions most infused with intention.

The more you feed the soul and nourish it with healthy actions, the more your actions will be infused with good intentions, leading to unity with your surroundings. This will undoubtedly result in healthy actions that benefit both humanity and the environment that provides us with a home. We must develop a core of spirituality to escape this disruptive, divided age and enter into an Age of Union. However, the boundaries of spirituality have to remain very broad. Even though we don't all understand spirituality the same way, we could align ourselves in our intention, meaning, and purpose in the world to achieve the same goal and help our species evolve in a way that is no longer fragmented. We don't need a new belief system; we need to create common ground, a spiritual base from which anybody, including atheists and agnostics, can benefit.

Spirituality is at the core of explaining life and creation: why we are here, what we see, how that happens, the unveiling of the process. Being aware of this process, then, acknowledges the evidence that we are all connected, in source and in purpose, and leads to an organic way of living in the world, with each other and the environment.

"The most beautiful emotion we can experience is the mystical. It is the sower of all true art and science." — Albert Einstein

Age of Union

THE INFINITE UNION

The mystical tradition describes connecting with the spiritual source of the soul as tapping into the unbounded strength and power of the infinite, endless light in which all souls are rooted.

To some, the infinite source of all creation is simply the vast expanse of the universe. To others, it is nature, or energy. To many Indigenous people, it is the Great Spirit. To religious believers, it is God, expressed in diverse forms but singular in concept.

However, regardless of your religious, traditional, or personal beliefs, as human beings we must acknowledge that the true nature and identity of the source of all creation is beyond the limits of our cognition. Though we are an advanced species in intellect, we simply lack the capacity to comprehend this infinite source. Over time, diverse cultures have found their own paths, symbols, mythologies, and theologies to describe and connect with it, and interpret its communicative devices. Yet there are so many more potential interpretations yet to come.

Mysticism teaches us that the source is both far and near. *Far* in that the source, from which the boundless universe emanates, is so transcendent that we as humans are infinitely remote and removed from understanding it. But it is also *near*, in that it is everything and it is part of all. Our soul, being of the source, yearns to be close to it, to experience it, and to have it reveal itself to us as we seek it. We can live lives of purpose when we strive to be connected to the source of all meaning, goodness, and love.

There can be no more powerful feeling than that of reconnecting with this infinite, undefinable, ineffable source. We can feel this in fragments, large and small, by appreciating its place in our lives; those moments of clarity, joy, and love when a spiritual wind rivets the soul; and those darker moments, when its strength is called upon to reinforce us.

An infinite soul that is
one with an infinite source.

A MYSTICAL ACCOUNT OF CREATION

In essence, all forms of human spiritual life begin with the narrative of creation. How did life begin? How did an infinite, all-encompassing source bring the cosmos into existence? The source, being infinitely expansive and preceding all concepts of dimension, space, or time, is thought to have gone through a constriction of itself in order to begin the universe.

A constriction of a primordial and infinite light cleared a void into which the universe that we know would unfold. Constriction was necessary in order to make space for a universe to be born —something created from nothing by simple intention.

From this intention, there came the emanation that we think of as all universes and creation, including the creation of our universe in the Big Bang.

Over the darkened void where a universe was to be born, a wind hovered and the source dwelled. From this place emanated every form of energy and matter of which the known universe is composed.

From a single seed of intention, every aspect of physical reality was born, and it unfolded outward.

In that seed of intention, all that was ever needed to create our reality existed. It is said that combinations of sound, frequency, and vibration—described in the mystical tradition as speech itself—emanated from the source in an expansion outward in every direction, radiating the known universe forth into the void it had cleared.

Sustained by the utterance of sound, frequency, and vibration, the physical universe was born as the source constricted and concealed itself, permitting boundless emanation. Light and darkness spilled across the void. Creation, emanating outward, was shielded from obliteration by the constriction, so that it could come into being.

As superclusters, galaxies, stars, and planets were successively formed over billions of years, taking shape through the laws of physics, gravity, dimensionality, and geometry, the seminal sound of the source sustained it. The utterance that emanated from the moment of creation formed and infused every moment of our physical reality, uniting all in oneness.

On earth, billions of years passed and a cooling planet became a cradle for life: an unfolding of reactions that would birth bacteria, plants, and animals on a fertile world of oceans and land. Two great lights watched over life on this planet. In the day, the sun supplied energy for growth and evolution. At night, the lesser light of the moon, planets, and stars marked the seasons of time, drew the tides, and reminded earth of its special place in a vast cosmos.

And on the earth, there was the still, the growing, the animal, and the human. The still: the stones, rocks, and waters of the natural world. The growing: the plants and trees, the grasses of land and sea. The animals evolving over millennia: the insects, fish, birds, invertebrates, reptiles, and mammals.

Millions of generations of life evolved over four billion years. Changes to the planet due to natural, evolutionary, and external forces resulted in dramatic recastings of life on earth. Over this time, five great extinctions came to pass. Species were lost, the strongest surviving and carrying the gift of life forward into each new epoch.

Into the current epoch came a new and unseen form of life: ours. Humanity was a step farther along in the walking story of life on earth, separating itself from the animal world. A differently mapped soul that reflected the creative nature of the infinite source, created in its image, created to create.

We are the sound of the source in our bodies, nourished forever in its infinite light, the daughters and sons of union and stardust.

WHAT IS GOOD?

We often categorize people or actions as *either* good or evil, based on a system of ethical, moral, or cultural judgements. From a spiritual standpoint, that which brings us closer to alignment with the source of creation, or closer to union, can be thought of as ultimate good.

Acts that create spiritual distance, discord, or dissonance, as opposed to union with the source of creation, can be thought of as moving away from good. When done with malicious or harmful intent, these acts become conventionally evil. In other cases, they simply bring us farther away from the union we seek and weaken our connection to the source.

We must ask ourselves: do our intentions, thoughts, speech, and actions bring us nearer to or farther from union?

Along the spiritual spectrum, activities that seek to bring about the destruction of that which has been created to share this planet with us, as well as activities that drive inequality, selfishness, and ignorance, can largely be considered spiritually distant or moving away from an ultimate good.

Here are some examples. Industrialized fishing practices that trawl the ocean unsustainably and destroy ocean habitat indiscriminately, wasting trillions of tons of non-commercial marine life as *bycatch*, which is then released back into the ocean dead or injured, is spiritually distant from the union of all creation. Hunting for sport also demonstrates a lack of respect and empathy for all of creation. Factory farming, where some species live their entire lives in dark, confined misery, is likewise spiritually distant. Not taking into consideration the balance of nature and abusing other species, the environment, and other human beings is spiritually distant from the unity of all creation.

If you stand with the voiceless and the vulnerable, those least able to protect themselves, you stand spiritually closer to the good in today's world. When we think about what defines good and evil, we must start thinking about how our own actions play out on a greater scale within the union of all things. When you think through the lens of union and act with spiritual purpose and empathy, you stand on the side of *unseparation*.

OUTWARD

Acts large and small, seeded with the intention of union, can bring the spiritual into the physical world, creating sparks of divinity in actions as commonplace as choosing to eat a plant-based meal or finding an alternative to a single-use plastic container. As we become driven by spiritual intentions, we open ourselves up to further revelations from the source, deepening our connection to union. This gives us the strength to be the positive changemakers we aspire to be.

Once we understand the intention of union, we will emanate positive change that will ignite the flame of global, systemic transformation in others.

Thinking back to the pillar of leadership, we are encouraged to become examples in large and small ways, and to use the change we wish to see in ourselves as a guiding light for others. Likewise, leading from a spiritual place and being a role model will help others in our communities observe and learn. Our spiritually aligned actions will have echoes and impacts beyond our comprehension, touching people far and wide. The ripples of our leadership will bear the imprint of our spiritual intention of union.

We return also to the pillar of culture, which recognizes the power of our different identities and expressions to enrich our lives and the lives of others, and to integrate concrete solutions into our day-to-day existence. Let us burn brightly together.

As we strive to reveal and understand the oneness and the spiritual purpose in all things and make real an intention that originates in the soul, we will notice the ripple effect of our outward actions and begin to see the first light of an Age of Union.

SPIRITUAL TREASURE

There is a story of the Baal Shem Tov, a Jewish mystic who lived in the 18th century whose legacy was democratizing the mystical knowledge of connecting to the source. In other words, he made this knowledge available to those who weren't literate, but who still craved a spiritual life. This was a time of great suffering, persecution, and poverty, when people needed hope. The Baal Shem Tov was deeply connected to nature and the idea that music and sound could bring people to a higher spiritual plane of perspective. He became known for dancing himself into spiritual states of ecstasy around a fire in the forest. He shared a story about the relationship that human beings can have with the source of all creation. In his story, on a day of joy, a king invited anyone who wished it to be granted a special request. This included taking anything they wanted from his palace, even treasure and jewels. To each the king gave according to their wish: to some, power and honour; to others, riches and wealth.

However, one wise person expressed a different desire. He did not ask for treasure, but rather to speak personally with the king three times a day. The king answered, "You can speak to me three times a day, and receive everything I possess." By doing so, the wise person chose the king himself, and with this wish received all of the king's greatness. This parable tells us that by choosing to have a relationship with the king, you will be given the blessings of the king. This is the true treasure. When you crave a connection with the spiritual, you are showered with much more than you could ever expect. Life becomes enriched with revelations.

This story reflects my own experience. Whether through ritual, meditation, prayer, or infusing intention into daily actions, a connection can be established that is accessible to anyone. We can all gain so much from such a relationship. I feel it is worth finding a way to speak of it that will resonate with and be relevant to anyone.

Spirituality can bring us purpose and meaning, and thus become an element of our own happiness. It is worthwhile to start looking at the world through a lens that can guide us to take the actions needed for change.

THE HUMAN PROMISE

Why should we strive to understand the origins and purpose of humanity? Are we not an evolved animal on a linear path of development? Do we not know where we are headed as a species? At this crucial moment, our very next steps will determine the fate of life on the planet. So, for us to understand our origins and embrace our promise is for us to properly balance our existence with the rest of creation and turn our intentions into reality. Modelled after the image of the source, we have the unique ability to connect our spiritual growth and the purpose of the source with our planet's future.

We must understand that our creation was a unique moment in the evolution of life on earth. We were given the unlimited potential to create something positive and special on the earth and thus evolve beyond our animalistic instinct for self-preservation. We were also given the ability to destroy. For this reason, it is our responsibility to understand the scope of our natural inclinations and, instead, synchronize our intentions with the goodness and love of creation.

In the mystical narrative, humanity ate the fruit of knowledge and awakened to our nakedness—our vulnerability—but also to our potential. This was the moment of the separation of self and spirit, of body and soul, when humanity was severed from the animal world. Born into the perfection of the garden, humanity would struggle with free will and the ego of the self, expelled to rediscover our divine source and the true nature of our soul.

A soul made in the imprint of the source, we have the power, intelligence, and means to form the earth. But we have to overcome ourselves, our urge to gratify the self alone. Our journey to reconcile self and spirit, body and soul, is a journey marked with lessons, bloodshed, and destruction.

Yet in humanity, the source had foreseen a companion in creation, and it revels in daughters and sons that cultivate sound and music, art and invention, design and language, dreams and function, delight and reflection. As our self-awareness seeks the spiritual, the source awaits our revelation.

Humanity is the only known species to seek answers to the unknown—we are the only known species that strives to understand the universe. Through our gift of intelligence we have pursued knowledge, and this has imparted us great powers of creation. In this way, we are a reflection of the infinite source from which all creation flows.

Though our modern desire to serve the self has brought darkness and separation, our artistry and inventiveness have also allowed us to bring our light into the world. By acting as guardians of creation, we can deliver on the human promise to bring our light into an Age of Union—with one another, with nature, and with our source.

Once understood, in our own limited capacity, the soul's connection to its source becomes the basis for our interaction with the rest of creation. As we deepen our connection and our understanding of it, we become unseparated from ourselves, from others, and from nature.

SPIRITUAL ROLE MODELS

Spiritual wisdom can come from diverse sources, and from this diversity comes a richness of perspectives and understandings. The writings of Indigenous leaders, such as Chief Seattle and Chief Dan George, have been a strong influence on my path. The unity between spirituality and nature in traditional Indigenous beliefs is a great source of inspiration for how we can *unseparate* our relationship with the natural world through a spiritual worldview of connectedness, respect, and stewardship. Within Judaism, the Baal Shem Tov embodies both humility and brilliance, a deeply connected person with a fervour for union and the experience of the divine, ignited by a mission to share that with everyone.

I look to the figure of David in Jewish history, a young shepherd who overcame impossible odds to become king—though not through his own desire. David's path was laid out for him by his deep relationship with his creator. In turn, the creator loved David's heart, that of a poet and a leader, whose strength was drawn from the source. No matter David's flaws and mistakes, he approached this relationship with joy and faith, and this deep love helped him through a life of great responsibility, victory, and struggle. David is an embodiment of the human promise.

On the day the boy David faced Goliath, a giant that all the warriors of Judah feared to confront, David fought him with only what was available to a young shepherd—a slingshot and stones. In this moment, his creator stood with him and filled him with the courage to face the impossible. We can all relate to this story. When the challenges of the world appear overwhelming, when the forces of destruction seem aligned against union, we can be David. We can face insurmountable odds with what we have been given: all is possible when the heart is aflame and we rise to our moment of impact.

Age of Union

Nature

Nature is our Mother. It is our connection with the great unity of all living and nonliving creation on this planet.

Our journey into civilization has gradually removed us both from the wilderness and from our base of compassion for other forms of life. The Age of Union is our transition to reconnecting with nature and finding our place within it and beside it. We must assume guardianship and reconcile our separation to understand and protect our living union with every creature that shares our waters, lands, and air. In this age, nature will be our teacher, showing us the way of respect, coexistence, community, and our interconnectedness with all things.

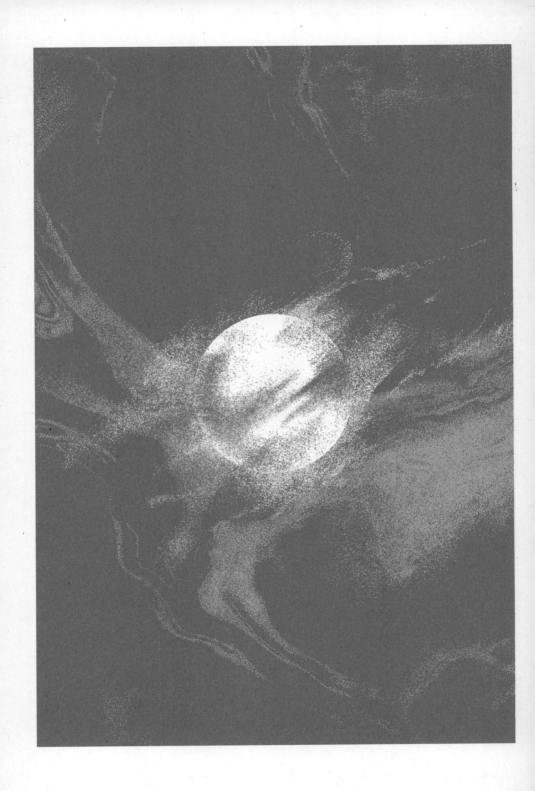

Age of Union

GUARDIANS OF NATURE

Humanity was created in a garden. This great garden, our planet earth, uniquely rich and abundant with life, has allowed humanity to flourish. As our myriad civilizations and societies have developed, our exponential hunger for natural resources has forever altered precious lands and waters, cutting deep and permanent scars into our landscapes. Today we tend to forget that we have built cities, suburbia, and industrial farmlands where wilderness used to thrive. And while nature is engineered to continually rebalance itself and its ecosystems, in this era the disturbance we have caused is so great that it has become our responsibility to care for both wildlife and its habitats. On this rich, life-giving planet, we must be on the side of life and guard creation with all of our resolve.

What does guardianship mean in an Age of Union? It means that humanity must make a fundamental shift from looking at nature as a reserve of resources at our infinite disposal to embracing our responsibility to protect nature and allow it to thrive. This shift is necessary in order to prevent our habits of consumption and pollution from making the planet irreversibly uninhabitable and losing all of the species, habitats, and life forms that contribute to the viability of our ecosystems. In this role, we will secure humanity's own future on this planet.

But we must look inward and begin making this change now. Our current generation may not be entirely to blame for the state of the environment and humanity's contribution to species extinction, but without urgent intervention, the impacts of such damages may be irreversible.

This change will come from the soul, from a spiritual place, from a vision of the planet in a better state than the one we inherited. This change will come from love—for ourselves, for one another, for the future, and for the beauty and majesty of nature that enriches our world and, in its totality, reveals its divine source.

THINKING LIKE A GUARDIAN

Nature has always been close to my heart. My earliest memory of discovering the majesty of the animal kingdom was a gift from my aunt and uncle: a two-volume set called *Mammals* by National Geographic. Learning about biodiversity around the globe and the threats human activity posed to all of these species developed in me a sense of protectiveness and empathy that only grew as I deepened my research and discovery of our natural world.

Growing up in British Columbia, with its abundance of wild natural settings and wetlands, within and beside the cities of Richmond and Vancouver, helped to strengthen this connection I felt. This love of our natural heritage turned into political activism when I made the journey to the west coast of Vancouver Island, at age 17, to protest the clear-cutting of old-growth forest in pristine Clayoquot Sound—a battle we won.

From there, I have followed a lifelong path of personal education, driven by a growing awareness of our environmental challenges and losses of species, and have sought to translate my growing understanding and concern into greater and broader commitments to personal action. Though my activism started with the protests in Clayoquot Sound, today it permeates all aspects of my life: from adopting lifestyle principles based on the zero-waste and plant-based diet movements to spreading awareness about wildlife extinction and threats to our ecosystems, producing a documentary series on lion conservation, and creating change in my own workplace. Concern for the environment has become an active part of my life because I believe that our actions, great and small, will make a positive impact on our path to union.

It's easy to get discouraged. Other people seem to share the same concern: why can't we do anything about what we are seeing happen around us? The truth is that we can. I know from my experience in business at Lightspeed and in creating social change at Never Apart that it starts with the soul. I know that when we connect to and feel empathy for our own planet and all of its creatures, we will align ourselves to come to its aid. Individuals such as Jane Goodall and Captain Paul Watson, personal heroes of mine who have worked to save species in our forests and seas, have single-handedly saved entire species from extinction. What if eight billion people decided to take action? It starts with me. It starts with you.

A few months ago, I returned to Clayoquot Sound, 25 years after the protests that shaped my youth. I returned to see intact and protected ancient ecosystems of old-growth forest, peat bog, and inlets with humpback whales feeding under the watchful gaze of bald eagles. The abundance of life I witnessed in a mere few hours is all the thanks humanity should need to continue our efforts toward conservation and stewardship.

During that period, the Great Bear Rainforest's protection from industrial logging increased from 5 to 85 per cent in northern British Columbia. And today the success of that campaign is inspiring other conservation practices around the world, including in Indonesia, where deforestation due to the production of palm oil is an imminent threat to the elephant, rhino, orangutan, and tiger populations. The Great Bear Rainforest could have gone the path of industrial logging, but a citizen-led movement changed its course. The same is possible for the rainforests of Indonesia.

This is proof that the actions we take today can have either a positive or a negative impact decades and centuries from now. The more we *unseparate* our environment from how we think and live, the more we will celebrate stories of successful and responsible conservation such as this one. We can find meaning in our daily actions and purpose in saving both our one and only planet and our sisters and brothers in the animal kingdom, who urgently need us to stand up as their protectors and guardians.

"When we see land as a community to which we belong,
we may begin to use it with love and respect." — Aldo Leopold

WILDERNESS

We have built our civilizations out of wilderness. As our home
and the home of a great animal kingdom, nature should neither be
destroyed nor exploited without respect for its intrinsic value.

In this age, our forests, jungles, swamps, deltas, and grass-
lands are disappearing or being degraded through development,
pollution, logging, and mining. They are under intense pressure
from the insatiable consumption and waste of humanity, from our
unceasing plans to develop every last remaining wild space, and
from our exploding population taking lands for habitation, manufacturing, and agricultural purposes.

Trees and plants bring oxygen and a life-sustaining atmosphere to our planet. They convert energy from the sun and bring the
gifts of life, food, and shelter to all living beings. We must see them in
body and soul, and respect their life-giving spirit. The more we study
trees, the more we are able to recognize their abilities to create and
sustain social networks. They share food among themselves and can
communicate distress signals through airborne chemicals in addition
to water and nutrients transferred via underground fungal networks.

Forester and ecology author Peter Wohlleben reminds us that
trees are only as healthy as the forest that surrounds them.[12] They
remind us that, collectively, we are all stronger. We should consider
trees our allies in our fight against rising global temperatures and
climate change—and help them to help us re-regulate this planet.
Forests have the immense power of removing carbon from the air.
And scientists[13] have now begun working on creating artificial trees
that can trap carbon and feed it to greenhouses to grow plants, emulat-
ing and amplifying these natural processes. Nature is indeed a teacher.

We should regard trees with reverence, but our land and soil
also have dynamic lives of their own that we should nurture and help
preserve. Without wild habitats, there will be no remaining space for

the other species that share this earth. Home to thousands of species coexisting and interconnectedly in tune with one another, wild places are spiritual sanctuaries for a diverse array of creatures large and small, each equally significant in the great balance of nature.

As the naturalist Aldo Leopold explained in 1949, we can either regard the land as a productive commodity, or we can regard it as "biota," which serves the larger function of balancing diversity.[14] This latter perspective is key to developing "an intense consciousness of land" and a desire to contribute to the life that it nourishes. Small-scale organic farmers the world over perhaps recognize best the intrinsic value of our soil. At the forefront of the permaculture movement, they may argue that monocultures are destructive because they kill the "living biota" in the soil. When handled with care, the biota shows not only great biodiversity but also great productivity—because species such as earthworms, insects, and birds all contribute to cleaning and fertilizing the soil, as well as stopping invasive species from impoverishing it.[15]

All natural elements have their part to play in the context of their biota. As one species among all others, we must play our part. We've come to think of wilderness as being distant from daily life, something to be artificially maintained and preserved without the trace of humans, and something we occasionally visit under specific conditions. But wilderness is all around us. Some wild and weedy patches in our cities can contain more biodiversity than a national park. This is important for two reasons: we must create conditions for nature to thrive with diversity, and we must recognize that cities are also home to species beyond our own.

---

[12] Peter Wohlleben, *The Hidden Life of Trees: A Visual Celebration of a Magnificent World* (Greystone Books, 2018).

[13] At Arizona State University's Center for Negative Carbon Emissions, a group led by physicist Klaus Lackner is developing a prototype for "artificial trees."

[14] Aldo Leopold, *A Sand County Almanac: And Sketches Here and There* (Oxford: Oxford University Press, 1949).

[15] In this kind of agriculture, there is no such thing as weeds. As author and naturalist Sally Roth explains: "The word *weed* is an epithet of purely human invention; in the botanical world, it simply doesn't exist." Sally Roth, *Weeds, Friend or Foe?: An Illustrated Guide to Identifying, Taming, and Using Weeds* (Collingdale: Diane Pub. Co., 2002).

Nature can teach us to be resilient. Wild flora and fauna can indeed adapt to and thrive in human-built environments if we let them. We see this every time we let an urban area go decrepit. When we neglect buildings, vines move up and creatures move in. When a neighbourhood in Detroit falls on hard times, open areas have been converted to grazing areas for goats and community farming projects. When New York City retires old subway cars, they're stripped of hazardous materials and dumped into the ocean to create surface-area-rich environments for coral reefs to bloom all over. The roofs of Berlin factories that have fallen into neglect are being converted into aquaponic fish and vegetable farms, requiring no soil and producing little waste.

If we can accept that these urban spaces are also partly natural, we can become better caretakers of the wild places that surround our cities.

"Where we live and work, we must learn to share the landscape —be it urban or rural—with flora and fauna large and small, predators and prey." — Emma Marris

We have to start thinking collectively about nurturing and protecting our remaining wild places, questioning both the belief that we are separate from nature and our consumption-intense culture that has brought us to this point. We have to step back and put energy and intention into taking care of nature. We have already taken enough. Wilderness gives us clean air, fertile lands, and ecosystems that we know our fellow species can flourish and evolve in. It is our responsibility to act before the earth's remaining wilderness is destroyed by greed and waste. We must act before it is all lost.

"Even if you never have the chance to see or touch the ocean, the ocean touches you with every breath you take, every drop of water you drink, every bite you consume. Everyone, everywhere, is inextricably connected to and utterly dependent upon the existence of the sea." — Sylvia Earle

WATER

The oceans, seas, lakes, and rivers of earth are where life began. Teeming coral reefs, dense underwater forests, living waterways—they all host a biodiverse bounty that we, to this day, are still working to understand and must cease to abuse. These waters have body and soul. They ensure our very existence, and are a precious home to abundant life, from infinitely small plankton to the whales of the deep.

Zooplankton are microscopic organisms that float in the ocean's currents. As the lifeblood of all biodiversity in the ocean, everything from juvenile fish to baleen whales feeds on these organisms, and virtually every marine species that doesn't feed directly on plankton depends on prey that does. These miniature ocean animals, alongside algae and bacteria, are also responsible for absorbing half of the carbon dioxide that gets released into earth's atmosphere, and we might therefore consider them vital to the survival of land species, including us. Unfortunately, pollution and rising global temperatures, as well as dredging, trawling, and deep-sea mining, are threatening the deeper layers of our ocean. How is it that the threat to plankton is not making the headlines?

We may understand our waters less than we do our land, but we must still take great care to treat them as we should our continental wildernesses. Today we look to the ocean as an inexhaustible source of food, without any concern for how our diets could be altered to help regulate and preserve it. Instead, we bring fish and seafood to the brink of extinction and cause invasive species to multiply. We use the ocean as a dumping ground for humanity's waste, our leftover trash, the byproducts of our manufacturing processes. Huge swaths of the ocean are now awash with plastic debris, polluting the cradle of all life, threatening our natural heritage, poisoning and choking our marine species and ecosystems. This is unconscionable, unsustainable, and uncaring.

Oceans, lakes, rivers, and swamps have value in and of themselves. They exist with or without us, and whenever we interact with them, we should leave as light a trace as possible.

Many Indigenous communities have made this reverence for our waters a central part of their culture. Today, some of their ancestral environmental stewardship practices are being used as tools to overcome climate change, such as selective fishing techniques, or *rahui*, in the South Pacific, or sustainable salmon harvesting techniques in British Columbia. Indigenous communities in North America and New Zealand are also fighting to have some rivers, which they recognize as their ancestors, be granted the same legal rights as human beings in order to ensure that we treat that body of water as the living entity it truly is.

We have both an interest and a duty to preserve the wholeness and sanctity of rivers and all waters. Their gift to us in return will be a healthier humanity and a planet whose waters teem with life.

"The summit of the mountain, the thunder of the sky, the rhythm of the sea, speaks to me." — Chief Dan George, hereditary Chief of the Tsleil-Waututh Nation and honorary Chief of the Squamish Nation and the Secwepemc people.

THE ATMOSPHERE

Protecting the earth and its inhabitants from meteoroids and cosmic radiation is our atmosphere, a thin layer of gases precisely balanced to support and sustain life. This perfect recipe is in itself a precious gift, a vulnerable yet vital few kilometres that shield and cradle our biosphere indiscriminately with breathable air, clean water, and tempered climates.

"Climate isn't really about some abstract, distant climate far away from us. It's about this air that surrounds us. [...] The air that moves right now in your nostrils. This air is our earth's skin." — Per Espen Stoknes

Human activity in the form of fossil fuel abuse, meat agriculture, industrial pollution, and deforestation have put our life support system at risk. As we know from previous mass extinctions on earth, climate change caused by a change in the ratio of gases in our atmosphere, particularly related to a change in carbon dioxide or methane gas, is the fatal trigger for extreme changes in weather that can lead to harmful impacts on our ecosystems and the life that depends on them.

From the worsening of air quality to the increasing frequency of heat waves and rising sea levels, not to mention the first climate refugee crisis, the scientific community agrees that we are already experiencing the negative effects of the damages we have caused to our atmosphere. Melting tundra and permafrost may release greenhouse gases long trapped inside the ice and bring about further unforeseen, cascading effects. The challenges we face will be compounded if we don't act urgently to reduce our impact.

Change in human behaviour and activity that impacts our atmosphere cannot come quickly enough. We must globally experiment to find clean alternatives to fossil fuels, explore plant-based diets that reduce the impacts of meat agriculture on our environment, and support efforts both to curb pollution and to halt deforestation.

While the challenges may seem beyond our personal abilities to make a meaningful difference, it is in fact our individual actions and voices that will determine whether we can stem a global behavioural reversal and reduce the carbon we emit into the atmosphere to our collective detriment. No challenge is beyond the realm of solution when we act together in union for the health and the future of all life on earth.

All is interconnected,
and dies or thrives as one.

"The least I can do is speak out for those who cannot speak for themselves." — Jane Goodall

OTHER SPECIES

A significant change of mindset regarding other species is essential in an Age of Union. Animals may communicate and behave in their own ways, but that does not make them any less sentient or mean that they experience less of an emotional life than we do. They have complex family and social structures, and deserve protected spaces in which to thrive. They have their own souls, with their own purpose and connection to the greater unity of the natural world. Living species have intrinsic value beyond our understanding.

Whether they dwell on land, sea, or sky, other animal species are not our property; they are not ours to use, and they are not ours to industrialize in factories like inanimate materials. They belong freely—in body, mind, and spirit—to the source, which provides for them in the waters and wilderness.

EATING WITH INTENTION

All living creatures must have the opportunity to see the sun and the moon, and to live their own lives to their greatest and fullest potential.

Where we once farmed in agrarian societies, we now raise and process domestic farm animals in industrialized indoor factories. Our expectation of the commercial availability of meat and animal products means that a vast majority of the eight billion humans on the planet demand millions of tons of animal protein weekly for their diets, resulting in the industrialized farming and slaughter of billions of animals per year. Not only is this environmentally unsustainable because of the amount of land, water, and resources required to operate on this global scale, it is inhumane. Were we to witness the lives of our fellow species confined in these factories, which are in fact hidden from the eyes of society, we would realize that the age of unity demands that we relegate these practices to the past.

The discovery of fire and the shift from a herbivorous and frugivorous diet to an omnivorous one aided our development as a species, helped evolve our brains, and thus made possible the intellectual progress we have seen in human civilization.[16] The time has come when our scientific and nutritional knowledge can help us to evolve beyond the need for animal protein in our diets.

Food is an essential reality on our planet. Meat requires more than 10 times the plant, land, and water resources that a plant-based diet does. We now have the opportunity to be nutritionally fulfilled by plant-based diets, saving lands that could be preserved or restored to wilderness habitat and putting the cruel realities of factory farming behind us.

It is easy to ignore human impact on aquatic life and marine ecosystems because we cannot easily see the damage being done by industrialized, commercial fishing and fish farms. Meanwhile, our demand for fish and other seafood in our diets has created an overfishing problem that is rapidly placing every species of sea life in peril.

A trawling vessel is indiscriminate in what it catches. It scours the ocean for anything and everything, leaving entire destroyed ecosystems in its wake. Billions of tons of ocean and sea life are extracted annually from our waters unsustainably, with lasting impacts.

In less than 50 years, the oceans will be incapable of regenerating what we take from them. Our fisheries will collapse, and we'll have brought extinction to thousands of aquatic species forever. The great oceanic life forms, some of which we are closely related to, will starve and dwindle in number, edging inextricably closer to extinction. It is time to take responsibility for these acts of dominance and connect what we eat with how it is sourced from the seas.

[16] Johan Goudsblom, *Fire and Civilization* (London: Allen Lane; Penguin, 1992).

THE LAST HUNTERS

In the Bronze Age, the human species hunted and trapped animals for survival and sought to carve out a place for itself in a world dominated by the existential threats of wilderness and dominant wild creatures. A naked ape, we employed fire and primitive weaponry to protect ourselves and our families, and to provide ourselves with food.

Today we live in a very different context. Let us accept that hunting and trapping other species, except in the case of personal survival and for the sustenance of traditional peoples, is no longer necessary. Simply put, it is wrong to hunt animals for "sport" or for "trophies" rather than out of need, with respect and reverence for the animal killed.

Hunting and trapping are not sports. Other species have no defence against the superiority of human technology and weaponry. We do not need to feel or support the egocentric sensation that some derive from the killing of animals, the mastery and domination over other species, with a resultant feeling of control over their lives. Have we not proven that humanity dominates this planet, to the point that we are now a threat to our own survival?

HORNS AND IVORY

One of the most magnificent examples of life on this planet is the elephant. This largest of land-dwelling animals, with its great intellect and wisdom, and a strong and beautiful sense of family, may go extinct in the next 10 years in Africa and Asia—the animals' long-standing homes. It is a crime that humanity continues to trade in ivory, the tusk of the sacred elephant, to make trinkets and decorations. Entire families of elephants have been massacred, by machine gun or poison, to satisfy the market's demand for ivory.

The rhinoceros stands on the brink of extinction, in part, because of the traditional but false belief that its horn possesses medicinal qualities. The last remaining wild male northern white rhinoceros expired in early 2018, dooming that subspecies to extinction.

Wild tigers number in the low thousands because they are hunted for their bones and skins. The lion, a great symbol of bravery and honour to so many cultures, is threatened with extinction due to loss of habitat, human-animal conflict, and trophy hunting. In West Africa, green turtles are hunted for use in medicine and traditional ceremonies. Even the giraffe, the peaceful and herbivorous gentle giant of the imperilled African savannah, is going quietly extinct due to trophy hunting.

In an Age of Union, we must revere all forms of creation on this planet. We must defend life and not contribute to the extinction of any species. That includes causing the imbalance of a species within an ecosystem, the removal of critical members within a herd or pack, or the dismantling of a family unit of animals.

Conservationists protect life; they do not stalk it and kill it in cowardice to feel a sense of domination. True conservationists work to protect wilderness for perpetuity, for future generations. Instead of a collection of trophies of the dead, a legacy of protected wild habitats, and future generations and dynasties of wild species, is the true legacy—a measure of reverence for life. The sadness and darkness of hunting and trapping cannot compare to either the exhilaration of protecting life, so precious and rewarding to witness in full bloom, or of sharing it with future generations through the sanctity of conserved lands. In order to have a place in an Age of Union, one should actively work against these impending extinctions and become a vocal and active leader in local and international conservations.

When a species goes extinct and its natural habitat is permanently gone, we lose millions of years of evolution and the richness and beauty of that species and ecosystem. But the opposite can also be true: reintroducing one species into an ecosystem can encourage other species to flourish. In Yellowstone National Park, the reintroduction of wolves helped regulate deer populations, which in turn led to growing populations of beavers, birds, fish, and reptiles, and to the strengthening of rivers. This is the power we have, and this is the kind of responsible dominion we should be exploring and rewarding.

THE END OF EXPERIMENTATION

Modern science and medicine have allowed us to live longer, healthier lives. Medicine has saved countless human lives and has helped us preserve the well-being of other species as well.

Technology has advanced to the point where we should no longer need to experiment on other species to advance medical science. In the most egregious examples of our selfishness, we see millions of animals live in confinement, pain, and suffering to test consumer brands, such as beauty and food products. Consumers have clear options for organic and non-animal-tested products. Lawmakers have the option to end these practices for good.

We must support and evangelize sustainable, non-animal-tested options. This cruel experimentation on our fellow species is something that we should understand happens in our consumer-driven world, and we must extend our scope of empathy and stand against it.

One of the cruellest practices in experimentation occurs on our closest cousins, the primates. Already endangered in the wild, with their habitats under pressure from development and exploitation, we continue to exploit whole families of monkeys and great apes for experimentation in many parts of the world. And while a few countries such as New Zealand, the U.K., and Germany have implemented a great ape research ban, there is no such formalized ban in the United States, even as the country is currently retiring all lab chimps to sanctuaries.[17] Nevertheless, a lifetime in a lab or in captivity for our sentient sisters and brothers is the product of our own moral failure, and this practice does not belong in an age of unity.

Wherever we have made the wrong ethical choices in our laboratories and production processes, we have a duty to rectify the situation and to rehabilitate the animals. This is a necessary step in making animal experimentation a practice that is forever relegated to the past.

HONOUR AND CARE

Our fellow species on this planet do not exist for our entertainment in zoos or shows. They are here by the grace and will of the source of all life, which provides for them in the wilderness and waters that are their habitats. It is our duty to protect these environments so that they can live freely, in their family units, and experience life as it was given to them.

Living beings do not belong in cages, and when we see this in any form, we should react from our soul with revulsion, knowing that in no way is it moral for the dominant species to engage in practices that are inimical to species that have no way to protect themselves from human exploitation.

The zoo is an obsolete institution. With the availability of global travel and ecotourism, high-speed internet, modern media, and high-performance cameras, we now have many alternative ways to experience these creatures in the wild and to educate new generations about the earth's species interactively. We must reject environments such as zoos and marine life water parks as relics of the past and return these animals to their appropriate habitats or sanctuaries.

Technologies that allow us to observe wildlife in respectful ways, and that minimize habitat disturbance, have made our viewing of animals both more entertaining and more helpful for conservation. Some great examples of this are forest bear cams and wildlife bridge cameras. We need to transform our personal curiosity for land and ocean species into an opportunity to document, understand, and preserve wildlife.

[17] Even the move of primates to sanctuaries can be stressful. "US Government Rethinks How to Retire Research Chimps," *Nature*, January 30, 2018.

A NEW STEWARDSHIP

A new relationship between humanity and nature must be formed—a new respect and reverence for our wilderness, waters, land, and atmosphere must be achieved. We must pay attention to the nature around us, be aware of our place within it, and be conscious of the wilderness that flourishes in the remote places of our planet, far from where we ourselves dwell. True respect and empathy will emanate out of a genuine curiosity for the lives of other species and a better understanding of our impact on nature.

For millennia, Indigenous peoples have considered all people, beings, and ecosystems on this earth to be fuelled with the energy of creation and closely linked to one another. We must learn from their teachings. Soon, we will realize that the care we give both to other species and our environment is not unlike the care we give to our own families and loved ones. When we honour our intrinsic connection to nature and pay close attention to it, each plant, each animal, each body of water becomes a living teacher.

Nature is our Mother. It can also be our mentor. It illustrates the richness of union and diversity. It gives us meaning and purpose on this earth in the midst of dark times. Nature has always held solutions to the biggest challenges we face. Why then have we not always turned to it to ask our greatest questions?

If leadership, culture, and spirituality are the catalysts of an Age of Union, nature is its foundation. From cultivating the value of connecting with nature to challenging our cultural preferences and behaviours, and thus ending cruelty, to speaking out about nature and the legal rights of living species and their habitats, we must embrace our responsibility as guardians of nature.

Every daily act can be an act of conservation.

Never Apart

Age of Union

Never Apart

Never Apart is our cultural centre. As a physical space dedicated to art and creativity in all its forms, the Centre has served as a landmark for the exchange of ideas, as well as a meeting place for people from all walks of life: diverse ethnically, economically, spiritually, politically, and of sexuality and gender identity.

What was my motivation for starting an ambitious yet undefined cultural project at the same time as running a growing tech company like Lightspeed? I was fuelled by a desire to make a social and cultural contribution to my community by allowing more elements of my authentic self to be brought to the table and challenged beyond the boundaries of my work life. As I moved forward in my journey and as my understanding of the world grew in step with greater understanding of my own abilities, I was able to make giving back a vital and integrated part of my path. At first I believed I would have to eventually choose between Lightspeed and Never Apart as both projects grew, but ultimately I learned that each project enriched the other. Both form parts of my authentic self and together they multiply my ability to make an impact.

We built Never Apart with the stated intent to create a space of unity and understanding, but in the process we have learned more than we ever anticipated. While it is still only the beginning, we can already extract learnings that can be valuable for any project or business leader. And I hope that the Never Apart story shows you that your desire to be a changemaker can go hand in hand with the many different aspects of your own journey.

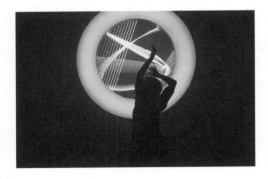

Age of Union

The question of how we would put our vision of *unseparation* into motion as a central tenet of the space was one that the founding members of Never Apart considered long before the first exhibition was installed. Specifically, how would the Centre use programming to drive change and develop leaders for change from within our community?

The Never Apart Centre opened its doors in the summer of 2015, in the Mile-Ex neighbourhood of Montréal. A former Lightspeed office, the company had moved its operations into a new space downtown, and an opportunity for this converted warehouse to become a hub for positive social change and unity presented itself. But we still needed to make good on this opportunity, and its potential and possibilities set our hearts and minds racing.

What unfolded over the first three years laid out the blueprint for a movement that explores how we may collectively move forward in a new culture of union.

Having benefitted from an LGBTQ youth centre in downtown Vancouver during the coming-out period of my early teens, I initially felt that a youth centre was a possible way to use our new space. This would have also actualized a clear mission of social change and unity. As we explored this thread, however, we gradually shifted away from the idea of a community centre with a focus on social work toward a cultural centre with a focus on gathering a diverse public around art, music, film, and discussion. As LGBTQ founders, we saw an opportunity to connect everyone through this project—to use our life experiences as connectors and to invite the artistic community in and allow them to become agents for positive social change. We wanted to create a safe space for LGBTQ and marginalized peoples, and also engage people of *all* backgrounds in a new dialogue to reframe the purpose of cultural gatherings around transformative unity.

The original team seemed drawn to the project by a form of spiritual magnetism. In the fall of 2014, as I was just beginning to think about how Never Apart would take shape, I imagined that

I would need "people like" Michael Venus and Anthony Galati in positions such as Executive Director and Music Director. From that intuitive spark, I was amazed to watch their involvement in the project take shape.

Michael was someone I knew from Vancouver. His art collective, House of Venus, had brought art, culture, and music to Vancouver's gay underground nightlife and had exposed me and many others in our early twenties to the performance, art, and music scenes of New York, Detroit, San Francisco, Berlin, and other urban centres. Anthony Galati was a talented, versatile techno producer represented by Montréal's own Turbo Recordings—a label that I greatly admired—founded by music icon Tiga. Within weeks of making this mental selection—my "dream team"—Michael visited our circle of friends for a Thanksgiving dinner at my home in Montréal. He was living in Toronto at the time and working on cultural and film projects for House of Venus. I had assumed that he wouldn't be available to take on this challenge, and had started looking for someone else with a comparable profile. I shared the intention of the Centre with him during the dinner, and to my delight, Michael joined the project. Within a few short weeks, Anthony unexpectedly applied for a sales position at Lightspeed. I met with him to discuss another role: Music Director at Never Apart. Along with Mike Durcak—Turbo's graphic designer—as our graphics and web person, Saad Al-Hakkak as our resident photographer, board members Kimberly Houston and Benoit Lussier, and Stephanie Marois as our French translator, Never Apart had assembled its core team.

We opened the Centre's first season with three original exhibitions that sought to communicate our vision and express our social and spiritual mission to the world.

The first and largest exhibition of the opening season was *Manifesto*. Photographer Qarim Brown had taken the original manifesto that I'd written—an expression of my inner, early intentions for Never Apart, which was infused with mystical language as well as environmental themes—and reinterpreted it as a photography exhibition and a video portraying dancer-choreographers Mariette Raina and Clara Cloutier in their search for being "never apart." They performed the piece together, bound by linens, moving to the words of the manifesto, which was spoken in English by Mikela Jay and in French by Stephanie Marois.

The second exhibition was *Colour By Icons*, a colouring book illustrated by artist Brad Firmino featuring iconic LGBTQ heroes —specifically those who had contributed immeasurably to society in times before an "LGBTQ community" ever officially existed. Their history—our history—is not taught in schools, even though these inspiring figures are role models for the people we were and those we may again aspire to be. Years later, works from *Colour By Icons* still grace the walls of the Centre, and our colouring room remains a main draw, where visitors can meditatively colour in the legends of queer history.

Our final exhibition of the inaugural season saw the creation of the *Moon Room*, a permanent installation by Kelly Nunes, Adam Sajkowski, and Oliver Simpson. This piece, a suspended globe in a blacked-out room featuring a rotating three-dimensional video map with NASA moon imagery, was and continues to be a quiet space for purification and reflection.

The moon has always been a personal totem for me—the full moon appearing at spiritually charged moments throughout my life and being a constant reminder of the presence of the divine and sublime in the night sky. As the moon affects our tides and cycles, so too does it affect us internally as it waxes and wanes—mirroring our own personal highs and lows, revelations and concealments. It remains beyond the immediate reach of our touch and understanding, a mystery and connection that I later found also resonated deeply with Michael and others at the Centre. The *Moon Room* and its eventual companion, the *Sun Room*, remain central meditation room attractions at Never Apart today—two great lights, one to rule the day and one the night. As one exhibition artist put it beautifully:

Our art lies between the Sun and the Moon.

We did not open Never Apart with the intention of establishing an art gallery, at least as we knew it, but intuitively followed a call to harness the power of culture to express our vision. Our first year of programming included the beginnings of what would become staples of activity at the Centre: art exhibitions, artist talks and discussions, monthly music events with an annual music showcase called *Equinox*, film series nights, a legend series featuring iconic artists, an annual wearable art runway show called *Wiggle*, and more. All of this has been documented in a monthly online magazine that regularly features video and text interviews with artists and guests, as well as feature articles by guest writers on environmental and spiritual topics to complement the cultural content. Eventually the video content produced for the online magazine would be edited for Never Apart TV, which debuted on the OutTV cable and online platforms in 2018.

As a cultural laboratory and case study for researching and developing the pathway of *unseparation* to a true Age of Union, Never Apart has also become a space for thought and reflection on the leadership roles that culture and diversity must play in building our future.

The centrality of art and creativity is ultimately one of the strongest assertions of humanity's role on this planet in relation to other species. Elevating and investing in culture has the unique ability to enrich life, offer forums for discussion and progress, and create spaces for diverse perspectives to thrive and be amplified. Through art, we hold a mirror up to humanity's cohabitation with the natural world, with members of our own species, and with the limits of our perception, capacity, and morality.

The original manifesto expressed our core intentions for the Never Apart Centre and provided a vision of the new culture we wanted to nurture. It captured the human experience, our connections with the spiritual powers of creativity, and the importance of building union within our cities, communities, and with nature:

ART AND CREATIVITY

Unique to humanity is our ability to bring art and invention to the world—the creative fire of the human promise to evolve into a species of wisdom that lives spiritually at peace with one another and nature. Art, fashion, literature, design, architecture, music, dance, science, technology: all are human gifts that come from the spirit to express our capability. These are where body and soul unite to enrich our world. Where there is darkness in humanity, let art and invention bring light.

SOUND AND REFLECTION

Music and sound are elemental blocks of the spiritual universe. It is vibration that sustains reality and life. Rhythms connect us to our source, and it is through dance that body and soul come together in spirit and union. It is in movement that we receive the breath and wind of the source and reflect its voice. It is in vibration that the soul finds oneness. When all is in darkness, let us join in resonation. Let us dance and reach our source.

CITIES AND NATURE

Cities, towns, and villages are among the greatest accomplishments of humanity. Our early ability to use the gifts of the natural world to create societies has made all of our progress possible. Let our cities become the greatest lights of our species, sustainable and full of art and invention. Let us build without sprawl, so that wilderness can coexist with respect, free of degradation. Let us support local businesses and farmers, so that we have vibrancy in the places we live. Let the human spirit build with wisdom and be a reflection of our promise.

COMMUNITY AND UNION

When our faith is lost, and the future has darkened, let us find hope in the communal act of building an age of unity. Let us depart from the path that has been driven by division. Let us never be separated from the spiritual union in all of creation. Let us cohabit in peace with life on this planet, where we consciously act to protect our world.

Age of Union

Lessons Learned

Over the past three years, each and every artist, exhibition, event, and talk has expanded our ability and drive to accomplish the missions we laid out for the Centre. In the examples to follow, I will present a few of these unique points of learning and share how we were able, as a team, to build important bridges, relationships, and opportunities as this cross-cultural project unfolded. They apply well beyond the walls of our own Centre and are meant to inspire any artist, entrepreneur, or community leader looking to help build a framework of activity fuelled by diversity, spirituality, and stewardship.

EXPAND YOUR CIRCLE

When we first opened Never Apart, we started by programming exhibitions and projects exclusively created by those in our immediate circles. Luckily, the scene in Montréal is artistically rich, such that we did not need to compromise on quality. Our first Equinox music showcase featured a lineup of some of electronic music's brightest rising stars, predominantly women artists such as Veronica Vasicka, Kara-Lis Coverdale, and Marie Davidson. Similarly, our Fierté (Pride) stage and Legend Series also spotlighted women, intersex people, and trans women artists such as Barbara Tucker, Candis Cayne, Mikela Jay, and Mink Stole.

It certainly stung when we later received criticism that, despite all of this, in our first year we hadn't featured a balance of women artists in our visual art exhibition programming. But the criticism was valid. We had neglected to expand our cultural circle to feature women visual artists as we curated our seasonal exhibitions. We had programmed women in music and film, but the limits of our early circle of gay and straight men meant that our exhibitions tended to skew male. We realized right away that we had to start reaching out beyond that first wave of proposals and expand our circles to fulfill our mission of being a beacon of diversity and inclusion.

We turned this critique into a rallying cry to proactively bring more women into all aspects of the Centre through collaborations with Nènè Myriam Konaté and Keesha Chung of CC: MTL, a woman-led group that brought young Black and POC (people of colour) into our discussions programming; projects with dancer Wynn Holmes and her LoFi Dance Theory sessions; yoga explorations with Steffi Nicole Goulet; guided sound meditations curated by Jann Tomaro; a special collaboration with the lesbian-oriented group Lez Spread the Word; and art by Eve Thomas and Richmond Lam for the Poster Boys exhibition. We took these small steps toward greater representation, which, in every way, amplified our mission.

However, it wasn't until we launched *Water* in the summer of 2016 that our first major exhibition solely featured emerging women artists. Julie Roch-Cuerrier, Marie Ségolène, and Tess Roby connected with our desire to begin a series of environmental exhibitions that highlighted our planet's elemental aspects. Collaborating with these three artists to create something new and unique to Never Apart, and which included a social and environmental perspective, resulted in one of our most successful and memorable showings to date.

By reaching out beyond our immediate circles, we found new voices and leaders within our community and, together, we developed our collaborative methodology and platform in the process.

Our core team, editorial staff, and board now include women who are at the heart of both our project and our planning, such as Music Director Leticia Trandafir, Administrator Sofie Tremblay, Video Editor Caitlin Gibson, Videographer Veronique Mystique, writers Emma Segal and Mariette Raina, and board member Bernadette Houde. Rounding out the team are Operations Manager Sylvain Brochu, PR Director Bradley Grill, and board member Mark Kenneth Woods. We are enriched by our growing multipliers of inclusion. To create change, you must make an effort to go beyond what and who you know to actively welcome new collaborators.

BECOME AN ALLY

The cultural mission of Never Apart is to *unseparate* people of diverse backgrounds through art, by promoting and spreading cultural understanding and dialogue with expressions of creativity. Because we have the physical space to host multiple exhibitions in a season, we are able to invite artists from different communities to exhibit at the same time. This is how we also expose attendees that come for one artist to the work and cultural perspectives of many others. Each season is a cultural celebration, and each art opening is a major opportunity to raise awareness and actualize understanding.

Because we present socially progressive artistic messages from diverse communities, it is important to understand how to be an ally to communities that you do not belong to. Creating space for these voices is imperative, but in itself it is not enough. In this regard, it has been important for Never Apart to learn the best practices of allyship.

Having the best intentions does not always mean that you'll get it right. But without the intention of getting something right, your project will doubtless be for naught. The road has not always been easy for Never Apart, but thanks to the patience and respect we have had for one another on each project, we have managed to learn the correct language, histories, sensitivities, and spiritual and creative sensibilities of each community and artistic network that we represent.

Our collaboration with members of the Indigenous Two-Spirit community is a strong example of how we have learned to connect cultures to create transformative, lasting relationships that can cultivate understanding and awareness to the benefit of many.

Two-Spirit is a beautiful identity for some members of the Indigenous people of North America. It refers to the non-binary-gendered members of Indigenous society, but the concept goes beyond the Western conception of LGBTQ. There are as many as five gender identities in Indigenous cultures, and Two-Spirit people have a particular responsibility to the lands and waters of their territory. They can play a special role in ceremony and bear a re-sponsibility to the spiritual life of their community. In the Q&A session with the artist group that led our first Two-Spirit exhibition, we learned that even though this term cannot be used by non-Indigenous people, it remains an inspiring example of how LGBTQ people may more broadly envision their role in society.

Kent Monkman, a Canadian artist of Cree ancestry, anchored the exhibition with artifacts of his alter ego, Miss Chief Eagle Testick-le, charcoal drawings, and a striking wallpaper of his iconic queer "western" illustrative narratives. He personally paved the way for four emerging Two-Spirit artists from across Canada to both curate and present a multimedia array of work throughout the Never Apart space.

Jeffrey McNeil-Seymour, a long-time collaborator from the traditional territory of the Secwepemc in British Columbia, exhibited *Unsettl(er)ing*, a dress representing murdered and missing Indigen-ous women, a social issue that has become a national crisis in recent decades. Dayna Danger featured woman-centric, BDSM-themed video and mask work. Preston Buffalo introduced his exploratory photographic work about identity. Fallon Simard showed acid-hued video pieces evoking the poisoning of the natural environments in his traditional territories in what is now Winnipeg.

Together, this body of work presented a completely new and hitherto unseen world to the Never Apart audience. The following year, it spawned several further opportunities for collaboration between the communities that had presented and, within a year, yielded a second exhibition featuring Danger and McNeil-Seymour called *Two-Spirit Man/Two-Spirit Woman Call Home the Salmon w/Help*. This exhibition explored how already endangered salmon runs are becoming increasingly imperilled by the looming threat of oil pipelines in Canada.

In an adjacent feature, we showed the film *Two Hard Things, Two Soft Things*, by Mark Kenneth Woods and Michael Yerxa, which chronicles the burgeoning Pride movement in Nunavut, a northern Indigenous territory of Canada. It examines the journey of the Two-Spirit community in this remote region, the intersection of Inuit culture with the Western conception of Pride, and the issue of allyship itself. Filmmakers Woods and Yerxa answered questions about how to be fully respectful and responsible when attempting to tell another community's story—difficult questions that many artists are still struggling with. However, by confronting these questions head-on with respect and open dialogue, we can use culture as a tool for union instead of further division.

A recent development in our relationship with the Indigenous community was the news that the 2017 and 2018 Two-Spirit exhibitions at Never Apart would be included as evidence in the national inquiry into Missing and Murdered Indigenous Women and Girls (MMIWG) in Canada. These exhibitions will serve to document the ongoing cultural dialogue among members of the Indigenous art community in reference to this tragedy.

The inquiry's lead counsel, Christa Big Canoe, recruited McNeil-Seymour's body of curatorial and academic work, as he is a Knowledge Keeper of the Secwepemc Nation and a specialist in colonial technologies and the continuing impacts of settler colonialism. McNeil-Seymour says:

"Settler colonialism is a trickster, a shapeshifter, if you will, that hides in plain sight, shifting and morphing into new patterns, unrecognizable to the dormant eye of the Canadian nationalist.

Age of Union

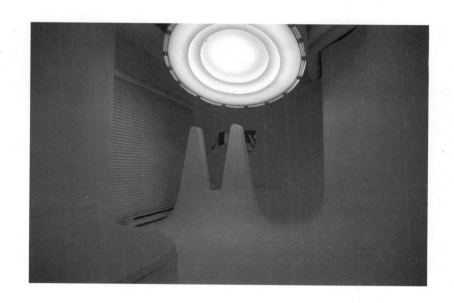

The installations at Never Apart revealed both the sense of loss and the urgency Dayna and I speak about, but most importantly, they also showcased what allyship and accomplice work looks like, and spoke to the works that other Canadians and Canadian institutions (like Never Apart) have been doing to be the solution—by providing space and platforms that help propel this message of resurgence and urgency."

Such a development highlights the power of culture and cultural engagement to create political and social action, and the power of uplifting one another to lay the foundations for new beginnings.

SHARE PERSPECTIVES
From struggle to survival, from resilience to irreverence, our second winter season at Never Apart in 2017 brought together people from many walks of life and prioritized the mission of sharing perspectives.

Among the most illustrative examples was the *Black Heritage* exhibition, co-curated by McGill University music professor and local music icon Andy Williams. *Black Heritage*, conceived to honour Black History Month, comprised sub-exhibitions as varied as *Serious Things a Go Happen: Three Decades of Dancehall Street Signs*, an exhibition of Jamaican music event signage collected by Maxine Walters; the *Assemblage* paintings by Sandra Brewster; and three exhibitions by the African LGBTQ immigrant group Massimadi, which included *Reluctantly Queer* by Akosua Adoma Owusu, *Erotes: Love, Sex, Magic* by Josué Azor, and *Limit(less)* by Mikael Owunna.

A weekend of discussions and panels brought audiences into direct contact with Black life in Jamaica and the Caribbean, as well as the area's history through music, while an evening of spoken word with artists Mutabaruka and Clifton Joseph illuminated us in the here and now. This event also featured a long photo slideshow by renowned black historical photographer Jamel Shabazz, whose vivid portraits and street photography presented a timeline of Black life in America—from the civil rights movement of the 1960s and

1970s to the crack epidemic of the 1980s and 1990s, and into the present. That weekend of Black Heritage talks showed the importance of bringing these different voices together to raise awareness about the diversity, complexity, and layers of experience of different contributors to this exhibition. Most of all, it resonated strongly with people both inside and outside the Black community.

PREPARE FOR CRITICS AND POLITICS

Never Apart has steered clear of being overtly political, choosing rather to be subversively transformational in its cultural approach. Although we believe in the power of using art to enter the political sphere, as this is where the conversations that are most likely to impact society, the environment, the economy, and equality are taking place, we also believe in using our space for inclusion. We attempt to present cultural ideas that build understanding between people, hopefully from all political stripes. It takes all perspectives and viewpoints to make up the tapestry of our world —intolerance cannot be accepted.

Yet today, wedge and identity politics are being used to divide people, leveraging populism and fear to influence us against one another. As a society, we've been conditioned to judge ideas from polarized positions antagonistically—that is, in terms of being for or against. So how, then, may Never Apart approach a politically motivated attack on its principles and programming choices from a place of unity? In the summer of 2018, we collaborated with a local festival to offer DJ lessons for women, transgender, and non-binary individuals during our weekly Saturday open house. As with all of our programming, the session was open to everyone, as stated in the opening line of the event description. Our intention was to create an opportunity for under-represented and under-invested-in groups within the DJ and electronic music community to gain technical skills, and our open invitation to all

Top photo on page 150: Screening of *Stagnant Pool* by filmmaker Kevin Calero, featuring artist Nico Archambault.

was reflected in the event's diverse attendance—typical of the attendance for our programming in general.

We were therefore alarmed to see a feature article, written by a right-leaning journalist, appear in the city's most widely read print daily the following Monday morning with the headline "*Interdit aux hommes hétéros*" (in English: "Forbidden to straight men"). The author used the title of our event,[18] whose intent was to promote inclusivity, to manufacture an inverted narrative in which straight men were being excluded and experiencing a form of marginalization in society. For this author, "social justice" and "political correctness" had nefariously entered mainstream social consciousness. The article received hundreds of comments and shares, which drowned out our ability to respond effectively—and which effectively silenced the normally marginalized voices that the Centre tries to encourage.

The author had tapped into a segment of the population that was receptive to such narratives, and people that had never heard of or visited Never Apart directed online hate toward the Centre. Unprepared for such a firestorm, we decided not to respond, outside of the comments for this article. By the next day, the author had already moved on, writing up yet another incendiary idea. We, however, sadly had to bring on extra security for the following week's open house. Many supporters did reach out to determine if the headline of the article was true, which provided responsible opportunities for us to set the record "straight."

We learned that one cannot venture into the work of social change and progress without attracting forms of criticism and resistance from elements that profit from division. But how we respond to unplanned hatred is of equal importance in our effort to serve our communities and supporters.

Every crisis is an opportunity. In the future, we must be better prepared to use critical voices to build new bridges in the face of division.

OBSERVE RITUALS

In our modern world, we have severed ourselves from ritual. Ritual once connected previous generations to wider strands of humanity and helped us transcend the mundane by invoking ancient practices. In an age where we have discarded ritual, deeming it anachronistic, we find ourselves lacking the gifts of history and purpose that ritual brings. Without ritual we are left, simply, with routine and, perhaps, the sense that our actions lack meaning. In this spirit, Never Apart has sought to create new rituals through our exhibitions and programming for those who might benefit from the bonds of social traditions and connection.

Practice is a guided sound meditation series hosted every month by researcher Jann Tomaro, in which groups of 50 or so attendees are immersed in a free sonic experience, which is unique each and every time, and focused on putting the mind at ease. Based on the research of Tomaro and her co-organizers on the positive effects of certain frequencies and sound properties on human brainwave activity, the series invites different artists to choose elements from their personal practice and rethink the way they perform these in order to enhance their effects. Taking place on Saturdays at dusk, these events offer a wonderful opportunity for participants to shed the stress and baggage of the work week in favour of mind and body realignment. For many, the *Practice* series has become a ritual of its own, a personal pathway to peace, and a new way to commune socially with one another and with the space itself through meditation.

Never Apart has many other recurring features in its program, like the wearable art performance event, *Wiggle*, which takes place in the spring, as well as the all-night music showcase, *Equinox*, in the fall. Additionally, our weekly open houses, film series, *Legend* series, and discussions are all means by which we're able to engage our growing community. Our seasonal art openings (known as *vernissages*), however, stand apart as ritual events that the creative

[18] DJ Workshop for Women, Nonbinary & LGBTQ+.

community has embraced, as celebrations of culture and diversity that are consistent in their ability to elevate those involved. Awareness, aesthetics, amazement—these elements embrace the vernissage participants, filling their senses with art that speaks to them and situating them within a community of people who all attend for the same reasons: to be filled positively, to be filled spiritually, and to be reminded of the human promise of creativity. Once a season, we join together to take a moment to affirm that art and culture can help us understand one another, and that it can change the world.

It was not clear from the start that creating meaningful and transformative rituals was in alignment with our mission to create a deeper spiritual awareness through culture. As we closely observed how our programming and events were being received, we noticed that our communities came to Never Apart not for the experience of witnessing a single exhibition, but to share in the momentum of building something over time, together.

Age of Union

Igniting
Your Project

The knowledge and experience accumulated in creating the Never Apart Centre can be valuable as inspiration for future projects. Ours was a concrete project to put the mission of *unseparation* into action through the modes of culture. Yet Never Apart was never about a single space doing what nobody else could or would do. In fact, one aspect of the mission has always been to crystallize our own vision of what this space should represent conceptually, develop its pathways ourselves, and then share our guiding principles to help anyone interested in starting their own path for changemaking.

The premise of this book is to understand the world through a new lens of union. An Age of Union cannot become a reality through the efforts of a few. Many diverse projects from a multiplicity of people and cultures will be needed to fuel transformation and align the intention of unity across humanity, society, and nature—igniting each and every changemaker across every project for the common goal of a greater union.

SETTING THE RIGHT INTENTION

The seed that created Never Apart was spiritual. The underlying belief was that art, music, and culture can nourish the soul and uplift individuals—not to mention foster community by creating a cultural dialogue between peoples of varying backgrounds. We didn't know how the Centre would unfold or how its mission would become manifest, but staying true to the core intention and not being afraid to declare an intention of spiritual awareness through cultural programming attracted like-minded collaborators and gave the team a clear direction.

One does not always get programming right, but missteps are key to learning—and it's important to view everything one does in a new initiative as a lesson. Once you've laid out the intentions for your cultural project space, your initiative, or your business, and you begin translating those intentions into thought, speech, and action, you begin to witness those intentions coming to life within a new community. As leaders of this new community, it then becomes your role to provide a foundation to support and make space for creative collaborators. If the intention had been to bring attention to ourselves or to promote our own personal agendas, the Centre would not and could not have succeeded.

A community project, no matter the form it takes, is an act of giving—a channel through which the team can enrich the community around it, nourish the creative spirit in all of us, and provide opportunities for a multiplicity of voices to be heard.

BUILDING A DIVERSE COMMUNITY

The reach and impact of your project will be greater if your intention spreads out to include a variety of perspectives and participants. Nurture diversity in all aspects of your project: the team, the programming, the audiences you cultivate. Nurture creators, both established and emerging, while maintaining a high standard of quality for programming and discussions. Bring together audiences that would not naturally gather and offer a safe space for conversation and reflection, ensuring that everyone feels welcome.

Make sure you stand firm in your commitment to observe all perspectives and amplify all voices. Keep an eye on the safety and security of participants and audiences. The social, political, and economic dimensions of a place will impact how the activities of an initiative will be received. Some places may have racial or gender inequalities, tensions between communities, or cultures of homophobia or transphobia.

Build your community around rituals. A project comes to life through rituals, which add a sense of belonging to a community and mission. The act of gathering to grow together and be a part of something greater can become symbolized in actions that connect us through shared experiences. At Never Apart, our vernissages, talks, workshops, meditation practices, and music events developed their own senses and meanings. These rituals became a core part of the Never Apart programming and culture, but rituals such as these can just as easily be a part of any project, whether or not it is organized in a physical space.

CONSIDER FUNDING OPTIONS

Until this point, I have been a patron to Never Apart. Having bootstrapped Lightspeed through its early years, I have learned that not taking external investment allows a project to bake in its own identity and DNA, so as to be able to expand and advance without losing its roots and core values. Having been blessed with the resources, the network, and the background to start Never Apart, it has been a joy to bring it forward and outward. Even so, the project does not belong to me or any one person. It belongs to everyone and is a beautiful composite of all of its collaborators and participants. It will grow to its full embodiment not due to the efforts of an individual or the work of a core team, but from the many people who embrace the mission of *unseparation* and engage with each other, united in a common purpose.

As one begins to conceptualize one's project or business, one will want to explore sustainable revenue streams that will allow others to share ownership of the mission and fully realize these important cultural, spiritual, and environmental initiatives. How can money circulate through an initiative that prioritizes human connections, the social good, or creative expression over generating revenue? The answer will vary by circumstance and community, but our investment in new ideas is one that we must make for our collective future.

EXEMPLIFY SUSTAINABILITY

Whether or not your project has a mission of sustainability, your initiative is an opportunity to use the lens of union to bring the values of respect for nature and our environment into its ethos. While Never Apart focused on creating change through art and culture, we also recognized that the Centre's greater goal was to expand our scope of empathy, first to one another across cultural divides, and ultimately to all creatures and to nature in all its elements.

To that end, we began to expand our artistic programming to include curatorial initiatives that shared perspectives on the environment and raised awareness on issues of ecology. We also took action in the setting of the Centre, partnering with a local company[19] to invest in rooftop beehives and exploring how to build out a rooftop garden, in addition to improving our backyard green space to expand the footprint of nature in our part of the city. We also became conscious about using reusable dishware and insisting on plant-based catering when renting our venue to external groups. These individual and collective initiatives can begin small, but they will expand as resources grow and awareness within a project develops. Making space for nature and minimizing your impact on the planet is a way to bring the values of union to your project and your neighbourhood, and to set an example by your leadership that may inspire others.

CREATING CHANGE AND DEFINING SUCCESS

Creating change and building social, cultural, and entrepreneurial initiatives is intensive work. Deconstructing social barriers, overcoming challenges and political agendas, and fostering a culture of empathy all require resilience, positivity, and faith. Never Apart, and every project with a mission-driven spirit and intent, must be a beacon that stands positively for what we are capable of achieving. The goal may not be profit and the outcome may not be monetary, but the social, cultural, or environmental impact may be something far more valuable than what can be counted on a ledger.

Leader, collaborator, or participant, we must all become seed planters. Collectively, we place hope in diverse cultural voices to carry forward our intention for union and positive change. In the greatest successes, we can see a future where we are interconnected, to the benefit of all.

The work will not happen without difficult days and tough decisions. It will not be without dejection, and it will not be without failure. To push forward is a calling and a fulfillment of our human promise. We can bring beauty and understanding to the world and illuminate it with the best of what we are and with the projects we ignite. A glimpse into such a world will reveal the growing shoots of our common efforts. These are the cultural and spiritual seeds for an Age of Union.

[19] The urban beekeeping company Alvéole.

Acts of Union

Change begins with our choices.

Every choice you make, and every action you take, can build greater union and change the outcomes around us. Every daily act infused with intention can help build the world we want for ourselves, our neighbours, and our future generations. Action is required. Action is urgent.

The following chapter is a list of 40 acts that will inspire you to start building, both individually and collectively, an Age of Union. These are inspired by the concept of *mitzvot*: daily actions elevated by a sense of spiritual intention, leading to "cosmic healing," as described by the Arizal,[20] a 16th-century Jewish mystic.

Some of these proposed Acts are large, some are small. Some of them you might apply and some you might not. Each is equally valuable and, when amplified or multiplied, will contribute beneficially to the world.

We must all take action. We must all envision the change we want to see in the world. And we must take ownership of our own role in making it happen.

Today we often act unconsciously—acting out of routine, without intention or compassion. We spoke earlier of the intention of union as a seed, one that originates at the level of the soul. Intention infuses our thoughts. It is then constrained, externalized in the form of speech, and finally realized in the realm of action. Actions executed with intent may at this point be separate from your daily routine, but through conscious work and focus, they will eventually *become* your daily routine.

We can only bring about an Age of Union by being mindful of how each and every one of our choices affects the world around us, including the people, the animals, the lands, and the waters. We should strive to make decisions based on how they strengthen and preserve the world around us. We should encourage others to do the same, without judgement of the individual path that each of us takes. We should envision ways that our collective actions may elevate humanity, as we collectively act to move the world around us in the direction of hope, toward an age of unity, love, and empathy.

Here are 40 Acts of Union.

[20] Rabbi Isaac (ben Solomon) Luria Ashkenazi (1534–1572) (Yitzhak Ben Sh'lomo Lurya Ashkenazi), commonly known in Jewish religious circles as "Ha'ARI" (meaning "The Lion"), "Ha'ARI Hakadosh" (the holy ARI) or "ARIZaL" (the ARI, of Blessed Memory [Zikhrono Livrakha]).

Age of Union

Explore a
Plant-Based Diet

Adopting a plant-based diet is the single most impactful way to both preserve and protect the environment, our oceans, wilderness, and biodiversity, and to focus on improving our health. Moreover, it is the most expedient way to end the industrialized farming of animals.

Just some of the outcomes of our continued consumption of animal protein (instead of plant protein) include the confinement and killing of animals, the pollution of our lands and waterways from factory farms, and negative impacts on our health. The consumption of animal protein is also contributing to the loss of our wild places and the extinction of species, since we require massive tracts of agricultural space to produce animal feed.

While not everyone can go plant-based overnight, it is becoming easier to do this gradually. One can explore this path by starting as a *flexitarian* or *reducitarian*. Eliminating red meat is an important first step and can have a positive impact on all fronts: the environment, animal welfare, and your own health. Next, eliminate white meats, such as chicken and fish, and begin to eliminate consumption of animal products, such as eggs and dairy, to become wholly plant-based in your diet.

More plant-based alternatives are becoming readily available every day. Each meal is an opportunity to draw the cause of union into your intention and bring about change through your choices and actions.

To try new protein alternatives
To support organic foods grown pesticide-free
To get to know your local market producers
To grow your own food

1. TO TRY NEW PROTEIN ALTERNATIVES

Plant-based alternatives to animal protein are becoming plentiful, varied, and more widely available. They are also becoming more visible as the public begins to understand the importance of this dietary shift. Protein alternatives vary from traditional sources of rich protein in vegetables and grains to new vegan "meats" and meat-like products that can help people transition to an animal-free diet without losing out on some of the food flavours they enjoy.

Americans eat nearly 10 billion burgers every year. If we replaced even just 30 per cent of the beef in those burgers with mushrooms, we could lower GHG emissions by 10.5 million tons of CO_2 equivalent yearly. That's akin to 2.3 million drivers parking their cars for good. Not to mention that it would save the 314 billion litres of water required annually for irrigation to grow cattle feed. And it would liberate 36,000 km^2 of agricultural land —more area than the entire state of Maryland.

While halting climate change and healing the earth require systemic transformation by the world's largest countries and industries, individual choices do make a difference. Pro-environmental actions—like opting for veggie alternatives—may seem marginal and ineffective when performed by individuals, but by doing your small part for the greater good, you join a larger pattern of behaviour that becomes self-reinforcing as more people join in. This is called a "virtuous circle," and ultimately it helps cement better social norms that improve the health of the entire planet.[21]

2. TO SUPPORT ORGANIC FOODS GROWN PESTICIDE-FREE

When we pick our foods, we can choose to spend our money to select ingredients that are grown naturally and free of pesticides. Not only are organic, non-genetically modified foods better for you, they also keep our lands arable, our bee and insect populations healthy, and our waterways free of harmful chemicals.

3. TO GET TO KNOW YOUR LOCAL MARKET PRODUCERS

To better understand how your food is grown and supplied, get to know your local market gardeners and the stories behind what they produce. Making a personal connection with the people that grow food for you and your loved ones completes the circle of awareness and can teach us more about how to improve our nutrition and health, while supporting the people who provide you with such bounty.

4. TO GROW YOUR OWN FOOD

Those of us who live an urban life have become disconnected from how our food is grown and supplied. Food is life, and yet many engage with food without a conscious approach. What better way to reconnect with the reality of food and enjoy eating like never before than by growing your own on your own property or in a community garden? Cultivate some of your own food, share it with others, and raise awareness about how what you consume is grown.

For North Americans, food travels an average of 2,400 km before it is consumed. For every one kilocalorie of energy we get from food, we invest nearly 10 kilocalories of fossil fuel energy bringing it to the table.[22] Much of that food comes from monocropping, whereby vast tracts of land are dedicated to single crops. This practice reduces biodiversity and frequently relies on heavy pesticides, commercial fertilizers, the use of preservatives, and genetic engineering. All these factors have contributed to the steep decline in the nutritional value in fruit and vegetables since 1940.[23]

There are other important reasons to plant your own garden. It helps stop soil erosion, which has made 30 per cent of the world's cropland unproductive in the last four decades; it helps to reduce nutrient pollution from artificial fertilizer, which washes into lakes and oceans where it feeds algae that deplete water quality for fish; and if you take up composting, you'll trim your carbon footprint and produce less landfill waste, a major source of methane emissions. And lastly, when you plant your own garden, you give yourself a gift: the gift of cheaper, tastier, nutritionally dense food. Join a community garden and you'll experience the added benefit of being part of a positive social movement that's hyper-local and impactful.

[21] Richard Waite, Daniel Vennard, and Gerard Pozzi, "Flavor Packed Burger Saves Many Emissions Taking 2 Million Cars Off The Road," World Resources Institute, February 22, 2018.

[22] David Pimentel, Sean Williamson and al., "Reducing Energy Inputs in the US Food System," *Human Ecology*, Vol. 36, No. 4 (August 2008), pp. 459–471.

[23] Tamar Haspel, "Monocrops: They're a problem, but farmers aren't the ones who can solve it," *Washington Post*, May 9, 2014.

Age of Union

Support
Animal Rights

Animals represent the beautiful diversity of species that share the planet with humanity and keep our ecosystems alive and thriving to the benefit of all. As the dominant species on this planet, we must commit to the guardianship and protection of animals from exploitation, and ensure that their natural habitats are preserved in order for them to thrive. We cannot reach an Age of Union if we do not extend our compassion and empathy to all forms of life. When we are able to protect, respect, and appreciate animals, when we are willing to stand up for the voiceless and the vulnerable, we will be worthy of a new age of true unity.

To be vocal about animal protection
To ban all animal trade
To ban testing on animals
To discourage the use of animals as entertainment

5. TO BE VOCAL ABOUT ANIMAL PROTECTION

As protectors and stewards of life on this planet, it is our role to ensure that animals that lack a voice are protected and given the opportunity to live full, rich lives in protected, natural habitats. We can do this by supporting local activists, environmentalists, and politicians who are taking a stand for such responsible values.

Factory-farmed animals live their lives in conditions of constant distress. They are kept in cages or crates so small they can't groom themselves, stretch, or turn around. To curb the high death rate, factory farms administer large amounts of antibiotics, which in turn contribute to the evolution of virulent bacteria that threaten humans. Wild animals, meanwhile, face different but equally grave threats. Human-caused habitat loss is a leading cause of extinction, as we eliminate biodiversity to make way for agriculture and development. Meanwhile, global warming and pollution are also critically undermining once-suitable habitats and harming vital food networks.

We need more people to help protect animal life. Farm animal sanctuaries are leading the fight against factory farming practices by rescuing and rehabilitating animals threatened by the meat industry. Consider supporting farms like the Sanctuaire des animaux de la ferme de l'Estrie (SAFE) in Québec, which cares for animals that would otherwise be slaughtered, or Mustangs to the Rescue (MTTR) in Oregon, which rehabilitates unwanted horses. Conservation agencies, wildlife refuges, and bird sanctuaries exist in all parts of the world—find one near you and pitch in.

6. TO BAN ALL ANIMAL TRADE

Recognizing the intrinsic value of all species on this planet, as well as their right not to be treated as commodities, hunted, or trapped, means that we must graduate from our current use of animal-based products, evolve beyond the culture of sport or trophy hunting, and support bans on the trade of endangered animal parts, such as ivory, horn, and bone.

Wearing fur shows an enormous lack of compassion for the mass numbers of wild animals that are hunted or trapped, or are confined from birth to death to create a single fur garment. It is selfish to subject sentient creatures to such a life for the sake of vanity. If we make personal choices to avoid these products and support companies that sell alternatives, demand will be reduced and sustainable, cruelty-free alternatives will begin to thrive in the marketplace.

7. TO BAN TESTING ON ANIMALS

Similarly, we must end the practice of confining animals and of subjecting them to testing and experimentation for any purpose. We have scientifically evolved beyond this need and today's technology offers alternative means for testing. Besides, many animal test results provide no useful model for predicting reactions in humans. Experiments on intelligent primates, our closest relatives, are the saddest form of testing. These creatures are the most deserving of our compassion and protection from these inhumane practices.

But change begins with *our* choices. The most effective way to ensure a ban on animal testing and widespread cruelty is to become a more informed consumer. Look up cruelty-free company databases to select the brands they recommend switching over to. You can thus prioritize labels that take the sanctity of every animal's life into consideration. You can also spread the word among your friends and loved ones to do the same. We can use our power as consumers to help end animal testing once and for all.

8. TO DISCOURAGE THE USE OF ANIMALS AS ENTERTAINMENT

Animals should not be used for human entertainment and profit. Aquariums are prisons that cannot compare to natural aquatic habitats and the river, sea, and ocean ranges that marine animals would otherwise be travelling over. Keeping wild animals in zoos and using animals in attractions are equally unjust practices.

Our respect for all life must begin with the elevation of our treatment of other beings that share this planet. We must aim to preserve wild habitats where animals can have freedom and self-determination. To achieve this, we can refuse to support zoos and aquariums, or other commercial activities that use animals solely for entertainment purposes. Instead, we should support animal sanctuaries by visiting them or making financial contributions.

Age of Union

Become a Conservationist

We must become aware and respectful of the intrinsic value and fragility of the natural world around us. Our biosphere sustains all life in our lands, skies, and waters, and sustains and secures the future of humanity. We must become guardians of our planet's health and long-term viability. We owe this to ourselves, to future generations, and to other species. In an Age of Union, we must become conservationists.

To join conservation efforts
To get informed about the sourcing of what you buy
To take part in urban rewilding and farming projects
To initiate a project for the environmental greater good
To be mindful of what you put into the ocean

9. TO JOIN CONSERVATION EFFORTS

We must join conservation efforts to set aside and protect in perpetuity the remaining wild places on this planet. In Pulitzer Prize–winning author and world-renowned biologist Edward O. Wilson's 2016 book *Half-Earth: Our Planet's Fight for Life*, he proposes "that only by committing half of the planet's surface to nature can we hope to save the immensity of life-forms that compose it."[24] To reach such a conservation goal, we can sign and share petitions, help raise awareness, and most importantly, invest in land and wilderness protection initiatives.

These combined efforts achieve three important, interdependent outcomes. They help provide suitable natural habitats for the species with whom we share this planet by permitting the free and safe movement of wildlife; they help restore lands that have suffered development, deforestation, mining, fracking, and contamination at the hands of humans; and they preserve ecosystems that keep the biosphere healthy.

This work may be difficult, but obtaining, restoring, reforesting, and replanting these forests, marshes, plains, and waterways gives nature a second chance to rebuild a lost ecosystem. In less than a generation, these places can once again be fertile and replete with life if we choose to invest in wilderness protection and restoration initiatives.

Stretching 30 km along the eastern shore of Nova Scotia, Canada, an archipelago of 282 small islands serves as a refuge for migratory birds and marine animals like porpoises, seals, and rare turtles. Called the 100 Wild Islands, this diverse coastal ecosystem has remained almost entirely untouched by human development since the last ice age. A community of fishers, ecologists, kayakers, and other committed citizens from nearby communities recognized the value of this natural treasure and committed to protect it. Since they launched their campaign in 2014, these guardians have been able to raise enough money and support to protect 85 per cent of the islands. Now they are engaged in their long-term care and stewardship for the benefit of all.

10. TO GET INFORMED ABOUT THE SOURCING OF WHAT YOU BUY

The internet gives us the power to access information to ensure that the environmental footprint of the things we buy is as sustainably produced and minimally impactful as possible. We can then spread information about our choices and help influence other consumers' behaviour to reinforce the support and success of ethical producers of the goods and services we need.

An example might be taking the initiative to research the impact that palm oil plantations or industrialized agriculture has on wildlife, forests, and ecology, and finding companies that offer alternatives to products from these sources. As we become more aware of the impact of different sources of goods, we can also become better at reading the labels that appear on our food. This may lead us to ask more questions about the sourcing of produce at a local market or grocery store and to become more informed, and therefore more conscious, consumers and suppliers.

11. TO TAKE PART IN URBAN REWILDING AND FARMING PROJECTS

Our own cities and communities offer unique and practical opportunities to reintroduce and foster nature through rewilding and farming projects in human-populated areas. We can choose to invest our time and resources into planting trees, creating urban gardens, and hosting beehives in places like rooftops.

Honeybees are the most generative creatures on the planet. They produce an immense supply of delicious honey and leave behind no destructive footprint. The only impact of their labour is that they fertilize flowering plants, including many that we humans rely on for sustenance. Though they have been bringing life and sweetness to the earth for some 10 to 20 million years, these diligent little farmers are now threatened by our herbicides and pesticides. If you have access to a roof or a yard, consider raising a colony of honeybees. It's easier and cheaper than you might think, especially if you rent a hive from a local urban beekeeping company. You'll not only be supporting a vital species for our shared ecosystem, but also the plant life in your neighbourhood.

[24] Edward O. Wilson, *Half-Earth: Our Planet's Fight for Life* (New York: Liveright, 2017).

12. TO INITIATE A PROJECT FOR THE ENVIRONMENTAL GREATER GOOD

Taking personal ownership of our environmental trajectory is an empowering act. Initiate care of your surroundings. Begin or join a local project striving for the greater good of our environment, such as a riverbank, beach, neighbourhood, or park cleanup. Involve the people you know and inform them of the benefits of this work. Lead by example, garnering new participants and support for the project.

13. TO BE MINDFUL OF WHAT YOU PUT INTO THE OCEAN

We must make every effort to protect our oceans and marine life by being conscious of what we flush into our water systems. What goes down a sink, toilet, or storm drain may end up in our rivers and oceans. Only flush chemical-free biological waste. Solid, non-biodegradable objects must be discarded so that they cannot pollute and degrade our waters.

Age of Union

Become
a Minimalist

We live in an unsustainable age of consumption, and to create a sustainable future for all living species that share this planet, we must choose the course of *less is more*. We must become conscious of the choices we make as citizens of the world, leaving a lighter impact on the planet and driving our economies in new ways that are less extractive through better, more conscious behaviours. Acquiring more things does not lead to greater happiness, and it does not move us closer to a better future. In an Age of Union, we must embrace the mindset of the minimalist.

To ban plastic from your life
To eliminate food waste
To limit unnecessary consumption
To buy only items that have a story and a real value
To use public, human-powered, or renewable
energy–powered modes of transportation
To track your carbon footprint

14. TO BAN PLASTIC FROM YOUR LIFE

The use of plastic has become prolific in modern life. Hailed as an inexpensive, flexible, and impermeable material that has allowed improvements across many areas of human existence, such as food safety or the manufacture of consumer goods, plastic has become ubiquitous. The challenge with plastic is that its use has proliferated across all aspects of our lives. The sheer volume of plastic products and their frequent use as disposable items have made plastic a major pollutant and a growing threat to the planet and its inhabitants.

Disposable plastic can be found everywhere across our lands and oceans, on mountains and in landfills, littering our environment and endangering animal life. Plastic particles, known as microplastics, also make their way into our bloodstream and cells in various ways, and we still don't know exactly how damaging they may be to our health and DNA.

Plastic is non-biodegradable, which means that every piece of plastic we create will endure for hundreds of years in the environment before decomposing. Only a tiny fraction of disposed plastics are actually recycled.[25] We can choose to ban single-use plastic bags, containers, and dishware from our lives and opt for reusable versions, or support manufacturers and products that offer biodegradable packaging.

15. TO ELIMINATE FOOD WASTE

Being conscious of how we source, purchase, and plan for our food must take into account the tremendous amount of food waste that occurs with every meal. We must return to the philosophy of taking only what we need.

Not buying food that will ultimately go to waste is one part of the equation. Being resourceful and creative with foods that are beginning to wilt, much like our ancestors did, and learning to cook with parts of fruits and vegetables that we otherwise tend to discard is a more engaging way to eliminate food waste.

Food waste is a bigger problem than many people realize. In Canada, 63 per cent of trashed food is perfectly edible, and the average Canadian household throws out more than $1,100 of good food each year.[26] In America, up to 40 per cent of all produce grown annually ends up in landfills, where it produces methane, a powerful greenhouse gas.[27] Europeans throw out 90 million tons of edible food every year, enough to feed the world's hungry more than twice over.

One sustainable strategy for combatting food waste is to boost your preservation skills. Learn canning and pickling to make your cupboards burst with easy snacks, healthy treats, and quick meal options. A simpler approach is to use the freezer. For example, don't let wine go sour. Freeze it in cubes and add them to stews and sauces.

Many chefs are turning their attention to helping people learn to cook underused ingredients, like kale stems, beet greens, and carrot tops. Turn juicer pulp into veggie burgers, grill romaine cores, and boil vegetable scraps to make soup stock. Some tricks are more straightforward. Vegetables looking a bit unappetizing? Use them in a soup. Fruit gone soft? Blend it in a smoothie.

You can also support companies that use food waste in their products, from beer made with wasted bread to beverages made from unwanted fruits and vegetables.

16. TO LIMIT UNNECESSARY CONSUMPTION

We can change our mindset from a disposable society to one where reusability and durability of goods is valued, rewarded, and reinforced by all. Our current practices, exacerbated by consumer behaviour and our attitude toward disposability, are incompatible with the goal of existing in harmony with nature.

Refusing single-use containers for foods and beverages, reducing the number of consumer goods we own, not buying clothing we do not need, or eschewing items we buy that might better be shared or rented for the number of times we use them—each of these actions represents a daily choice we can make to reduce our environmental impact while still maintaining a high standard of living.

[25] According to the Royal Statistical Society, 90.5% of plastic waste has not been recycled. Royal Statistical Society, "Statistics of the Year 2018: Winners Announced," *Statslife.org.uk*, December 17, 2018.

[26] Magdaline Boutros, "New National Campaign Launched to Reduce Household Food Waste," *Globe and Mail*, July 18, 2018.
[27] Dana Gunders, "Wasted: How America is Losing up to 40 Percent of Its Food from Farm to Fork to Landfill," *NRDC.org*, August 16, 2017.

We should strive to achieve a zero-waste lifestyle wherein our consumer choices are infused with the intention to conserve and recycle our resources, eliminate waste, and protect our planet.

17. TO BUY ONLY ITEMS THAT HAVE A STORY AND A REAL VALUE

In cases where we need an item, we should make every effort to buy discretionary items that have a real story of sustainability or a social mission, such that our consumer choices themselves aid in creating good. When we buy, we must ensure that we are able to repurpose an item by being able to reuse or share it. We must also develop the habit of repairing and maintaining what we already own.

18. TO USE PUBLIC, HUMAN-POWERED, OR RENEWABLE ENERGY-POWERED MODES OF TRANSPORTATION

Human-powered modes of transportation such as walking and biking in our urban centres are the no-impact choice for getting from one place to another. When we need to cover larger distances, public transportation such as subways, trams, and buses is a way to share the impact. By demanding that such modes of transportation be powered by renewable energy, we can effect great change.

Electric or renewable-energy vehicles are also an investment we can make to ensure that personal transportation over larger distances is compatible with our goals for protecting our atmosphere and slowing—and eventually halting—the devastating effects of climate change. Where possible, we should employ carpooling and ridesharing to further optimize our use of resources for the benefit of our planet.

Biking to work saves money, promotes health, and even makes you smarter, according to recent studies. It also makes the planet a nicer place for others. Drivers release on average 0.75 pounds of carbon dioxide per kilometre, while cyclists release only 0.4 grams—through their sweat! Be generous with your perspiration; it's a small step that counts.[28]

Age of Union

19. TO TRACK YOUR CARBON FOOTPRINT

Carbon is an abstract concept for many of us, but its prolonged presence in the atmosphere contributes immensely to the "greenhouse effect," leading to global warming and the damage we are witnessing due to climate change. Thankfully, though, we are now able to visualize our individual ecological footprints using online carbon calculators.

Finding out how much carbon we contribute to the atmosphere in our lives daily and yearly is a first step that we can take toward reducing our personal impact, whether that means cutting down on air travel and limiting car usage, composting and reducing landfill waste, or finding ways to save energy and electricity. Join the fight against climate change by beginning to track your progress and learning how to make daily choices to reduce your carbon footprint.

[28] Laura McCamy, "How Green is Your Bike?," *Momentum Mag*, April 27, 2015.

Nourish Your Body and Soul

We must invest in our own abilities to be changemakers by nourishing the body and the soul. We nourish our bodies in response to hunger and thirst, but the soul also yearns to be nourished. Devoting time to learning about and deepening our understanding of our spiritual identity will bring meaning into our lives, because the soul is the part of us that is most closely connected to the greater unity of all things.

The soul's partner in action is the body. Together they unite the spiritual with the physical by bringing the seed of the soul's intention into the realities of thought, speech, and action. It is therefore imperative that we nourish our bodies in alignment with our souls, to enable them to be vital instruments for change and transformation in our physical world.

To practice a physical activity every day
To cook every week
To read and expand your worldview
To meditate daily
To partake in or create new rituals for yourself and to share in rituals with your friends, family, and community
To spend more time outdoors
To speak your mind
To become a better listener
To set aside time for spiritual development

20. TO PRACTICE PHYSICAL ACTIVITY EVERY DAY

Set aside time each week to be active and regenerate your health through exercise—anything from walking outside to team sports, yoga, martial arts, running, and swimming, to working up a sweat in a studio or a gym.

We connect with our body through physical activity and we strengthen its ability to act on behalf of change. The millennia-old practice of yoga is a great example of how a physical activity can intensify the connection between body and soul.

21. TO COOK EVERY WEEK

Nourishing your body begins with how you fuel it. A plant-based and organic diet supplies the body with nutrients. It also reinforces our respect for our life, our health, and the life and health of the planet. Cooking for yourself and your loved ones not only nourishes your body, it also creates a connection with the food you consume and an age-old connection with others in an act of giving and sharing, and potentially less food waste and discarded packaging. A diverse and well-researched diet can help both your body and mind operate at peak capacity.

22. TO READ AND EXPAND YOUR WORLDVIEW

In order to be an agent of change, it is important to be well-informed and well aware of the wealth of human experience and how our world works. Reading about human history, geography, spirituality, and culture, as well as engaging with works of fiction and nonfiction alike, are key to knowing how to contribute positively to this world.

Understanding the expansive mechanics of our world and the bounty of creative thought gifted to us from generations past will help you feel better connected to the story of humanity and to gain a better sense of the value of protecting our planet.

23. TO MEDITATE DAILY

Meditation is within everyone's reach. It is the place where the body and the soul encounter one another, the place where they reunite. It takes only a few minutes. Anyone can sit and feel what is happening, feel the body, and feel the gift of breath. Take a quiet moment to experience the soul. This is where it starts; it's as simple as that.

24. TO PARTAKE IN OR CREATE RITUALS FOR YOURSELF AND SHARE RITUALS WITH YOUR FRIENDS, FAMILY, AND COMMUNITY

To break up daily and weekly routines, we can infuse our days with meaning and purpose by partaking in both personal rituals and rituals we share with our loved ones and our community. These may be physical or spiritual acts, acts of giving, or new traditions that deepen our connections. Rituals can vary from a meditation, mantra, or prayer to a weekly gathering or discussion on topics concerning our community, to an annual journey to a place of inspiration and spiritual regeneration. Anything that brings you closer to your ancestors, to your traditional heritage, or to your loved ones is worth transforming into a ritual.

25. TO SPEND MORE TIME OUTDOORS

In the modern world, we spend much of our time indoors in the home, at work, and at social gatherings, as well as an ever-increasing amount of time in virtual spaces like the internet, social media and screen-based games. This is isolating. Making an effort to spend more time outdoors and in nature will help unite you with the world at large and deepen your appreciation of nature in all its wild beauty.

> Hang out with trees. The Japanese practice of *shinrin-yoku* (spending time in the forest or "forest bathing") has been proven to reduce cortisol levels—a hormone that indicates stress—and sympathetic nervous activity, which is associated with the fight-or-flight response. In other words, nature calms us down. Not only that, studies have demonstrated that it also improves short-term memory, boosts the immune system, and even augments creative problem-solving abilities. So if you want to find your most calm and generative state of mind, get out of the city and take a soak in the woods.

26. TO SPEAK YOUR MIND

We often speak without consciously thinking about either the intent or impact of our words. When we proceed from an intention of union, our thoughts become rich with understanding, empathy, and respect. Becoming cognizant of the process of constricting those ideas into carefully chosen words, and forming and then delivering one's words as speech, can lead to positive communication and positive action. You should not be afraid to speak your mind, whether through speech or writing, if you have positive and heartfelt intentions.

27. TO BECOME A BETTER LISTENER

We have explored how intention leads first to thought, then speech, and finally completes its journey in action. A key part of integrating greater understanding and empathy toward others into our way of being is through the act of listening. In listening to others when they speak, you have an opportunity to understand and benefit from their perspective. Listening is the act of giving one's attention and respect to another—it fosters trust and communication and creates fertile ground for collaboration.

28. TO SET ASIDE TIME FOR SPIRITUAL DEVELOPMENT

The concept of the sacred place is well established. It is where one goes to have a moment of spiritual respite from the world. The concept of sacred time is just as important. You can take a moment for spirituality anywhere when you set aside time in your week to focus on your own spiritual development.

In the Jewish tradition, this is called *Shabbat*. Lasting for 24 hours from sundown on Friday to sundown on Saturday, time itself is set aside to rest and develop one's spiritual sensibilities through reading, meditation, prayer, spending quality time with loved ones, or giving back to one's community. You can similarly find time in your weekly routine to remove yourself from the world of work and electronic screen-time to nourish your soul, connect with your source, and become a more centred person.

13 scientifically proven ways in which meditation heals the body[29]

It reduces anxiety.
It decreases depression
in the short and long term.
It helps you feel better
about yourself.
It reduces cognitive rigidity and
cultivates creative problem solving.
It strengthens your ability
to concentrate and focus.
It improves memory.
It reduces age-related
cognitive decline.
It reduces inflammation
from stress.
It increases compassion
toward yourself and others.
It helps control anger
and avoid conflict.
It helps you sleep better.
It helps you control
addictive cravings.
It lowers your blood pressure.

[29] Multiple sources: *Journal of Behavioral Medicine* (2008); *Psychosomatics* (2015); *General Hospital Psychiatry* (1995); *Supportive Care Cancer* (2005); *Cognitive, Affective, and Behavioral Neuroscience* (2007); *Journal of Alzheimer's Disease* (2015); *Brain, Behavior, and Immunity* (2013); *Journal of Consulting and Clinical Psychology* (2014); *Clinical Psychology Review* (2011); *Current Opinion in Pulmonary Medicine* (2015).

Age of Union

Embrace Your Community

We cannot bring about an Age of Union in isolation. Union means that we understand and have joined the greater community while remaining open to the diversity of humanity and of the species we share the planet with. We must also engage with our local community, an important milieu for the aspiring changemaker. This is where we can directly observe the impacts of our efforts and be models for change for those around us by contributing, learning, and building empathy in ways that can then influence and reverberate through the communities of the world.

To get to know a local entrepreneur
To support local art, music, and culture
To start volunteering
To fund worthy causes
To become a mentor to a younger person
To join online groups with a positive impact
To share resources with your neighbours
To run an ethical, environmentally conscious business or organization
To embrace people in all their diversity
To support education in all its forms
To seek out the knowledge of elders
To always vote

29. TO GET TO KNOW A LOCAL ENTREPRENEUR

Your actions can also have a financial impact on your community. For example, shopping and dining at local independent businesses can help circulate funds in your local economy, support employment, and provide residual benefits to families touched by that business. Independent retailers, restaurateurs, and food vendors may then be empowered to make enlightened choices on sourcing, prioritizing ethical and sustainable suppliers to a greater degree than multinational corporations and franchise chains can.

Get to know your local entrepreneurs. They may already be business owners in your neighbourhood or creating new business models that strive to move us closer to union. Local entrepreneurs are both accountable to their local communities and able to lead us to make better choices for our safety and health, and for the health of the planet.

30. TO SUPPORT LOCAL ART, MUSIC, AND CULTURE

Art, music, and culture are the sweetest fruits of humanity. These expressions of beauty and truth have the power to enrich our lives but require everyone's support in order to thrive. The ability to create is a mirror of the source of creation. Our creativity should therefore be celebrated and enjoyed by everyone, and you may find great joy in making the creative arts available to all.

When we support our artists, musicians, filmmakers, dancers, designers, and other creatives, we bring beauty into our lives and cities, enriching the world for everyone. We also allow these individuals to follow their calling, to be a voice to raise awareness on matters that affect us all.

Start to engage by being curious about people's creative and artistic endeavours: actively visit exhibitions and performances of unfamiliar local artists, support their practice by buying their work or recommending it to friends, and encourage creative people you know in pushing the boundaries of their craft.

31. TO START VOLUNTEERING

In volunteering, one offers the precious gift of one's own time for the benefit of others and the greater good. It is an act of selflessness that is its own reward. Helping those less fortunate, sharing with those in need of our knowledge, or elevating our planet and its species are worthwhile ways to share of our time and abilities. Take on even a single volunteer task to begin the journey of giving.

32. TO FUND WORTHY CAUSES

Worthy causes require our commitment and investment. We can give of our own financial and material resources to support causes that help others in need, or species and ecosystems that require our support. Many projects lack human capital as well, but even when there are ready helpers, funding is the necessary fuel to develop and sustain the ability to do good work in the world. In being a source of funding, we convert our personal earnings into an impactful act of giving and positive change.

33. TO BECOME A MENTOR TO A YOUNGER PERSON

We are educated as individuals by the role models that inspire us. Give back by becoming a mentor to a younger person. Be a sounding board for their ideas and aspirations. Be a foundation of support for their personal development. Mentorship is a gift that we all can give, and as we accumulate wisdom and knowledge in this life, it is a gift that we can share.

Perhaps the most powerful aspect of mentorship is that it's a two-way street. Both parties can learn, grow, and elevate one another toward a greater union.

34. TO JOIN ONLINE GROUPS WITH A POSITIVE IMPACT

We can fill our news feeds with positivity and learning by joining online groups that seek to make a positive impact and spread information to create a world filled with the intention of union. Join groups on how to adopt plant-based diets, environmentally conscious solutions, zero-waste lifestyles, animal protection, and wilderness conservation. Join groups that explore and teach about cultures other than your own. Share content that will spark awareness in your network. Action begins with positive and progressive thought.

35. TO SHARE RESOURCES WITH YOUR NEIGHBOURS

Much has been said about the so-called sharing and gig economies. To reduce overconsumption and maximize the responsible, sustainable use of our existing resources, it's important to get to know your neighbours and fellow community members through sharing or pooling what you already collectively own. By reinforcing a collective culture of reuse, you will aid in creating richer personal connections and stronger local support networks, and leave a lighter imprint on our planet.

> Consider joining or starting a Food is Free project. Their mission is to help people take back their food security and meet their neighbours. If you have a front yard or know of an unused public space, Food is Free shows you how to use salvaged materials to build a low-maintenance garden that only needs to be watered every two to four weeks, so you can start growing organic food without much effort. Share the harvest, and you'll see your neighbourhood become a stronger and more connected community. Take it to the next level by hosting potlucks, composting together, and starting a tool-sharing program.

36. TO RUN AN ETHICAL, ENVIRONMENTALLY CONSCIOUS BUSINESS OR ORGANIZATION

As a business owner or employee, no matter the scale or industry, you can foster leadership by using the workplace to drive equality and sustainability as key values every day. Companies and organizations on all levels have as much responsibility for the well-being of a society and the planet as individuals and governments.

Your business or organization can mandate sustainability in how you source materials, products, and supplies, as well as how you use those resources in your operations to reduce waste. You can build the values of equality and diversity into your hiring practices and career path, recognizing that when a company includes many diverse perspectives and voices, it has the potential both to produce better and smarter solutions and to lead by example.

Paying living wages and providing benefits is not always easy as a starting entrepreneur, but it's an impressive goal, as this commitment enables workers to provide for themselves and their families. It also empowers individuals to become leaders on their own path to making positive change.

37. TO EMBRACE PEOPLE IN ALL THEIR DIVERSITY

Understanding the collective contributions of the many different cultures and communities on this earth is key to bringing about positive global change. Having many different perspectives at the table and including more diversity will lead us to better, stronger solutions for common struggles and goals.

The best way to understand one another, develop empathy for one another, shatter echo chambers, and be able to work collectively for union is to learn about human diversity, learn about people who aren't like us, and bridge differences in understanding with an open heart.

Start by looking beyond your immediate circles and befriending and growing your understanding of other people. Bringing others that are different from you into your life, your social community, and your workplace is enriching on a personal level and will create bonds that are truly necessary for ushering in an Age of Union. Remember to approach new and unfamiliar cultural communities with wholehearted respect.

38. TO SUPPORT EDUCATION IN ALL ITS FORMS

Education is key to growing our collective awareness and to understanding one another and the world. You can make a personal commitment to your own education through reading and schooling, but you can also ensure continued support for educational institutions and libraries through personal financial contributions or time spent volunteering. When you support educational programs, you support uplifting people whom you may never even meet by enhancing the spread of knowledge and cultivating a society that is aware of and ready for change through union.

39. TO SEEK OUT THE KNOWLEDGE OF ELDERS

Our elders are invaluable sources of wisdom and learning. They can be sounding boards for our own ideas and guide us in the challenges we face as developing changemakers. Your elders have themselves been changemakers, and when you engage with them, you learn to be a better citizen and agent for changemaking.

40. TO ALWAYS VOTE

There is so much you can do on a personal level to bring union into this world, but taking an active part in our political system by voting to elect leaders that represent your values and who will work in the interest of all people, our planet, and its species is key to catalyzing the broad changes you want to see in the world. Our governments will frustrate us at times, and elected officials will make decisions that we feel are unaligned with our vision of a unified world, so it is also our responsibility to use the power of the vote to voice our opinions. We must become and remain personally involved in the political process to bring positive change to our world.

Conclusion

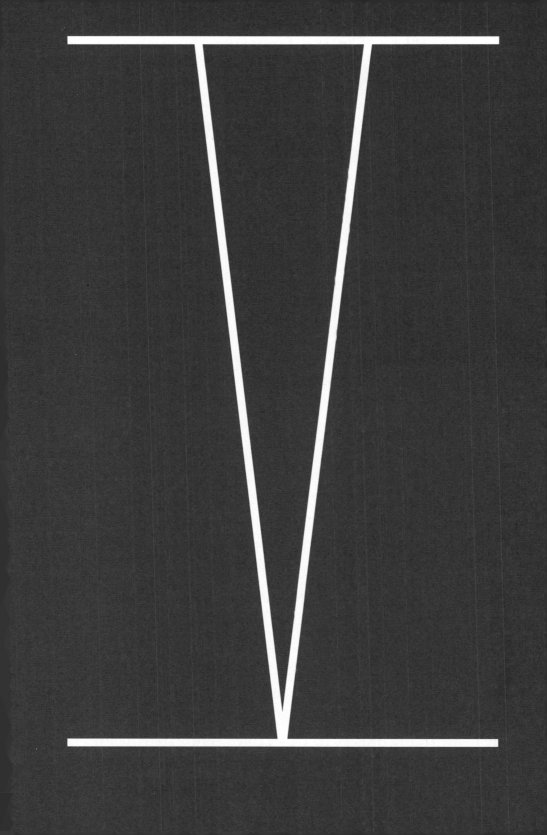

Live to Bring Forth
an Age of Union

We have all of the tools, resources, mass communication technologies, and desire we need to initiate a new direction for human life on this planet. As individuals, we are each uniquely gifted and driven to fulfill our personal life goals. We all want to feel successful in bringing forth our talents, making good on opportunities to enhance ourselves, and contributing positively to this world.

To these personal goals we must add an attentive focus upon the greater good. We are at a turning point in the trajectory of our species. Our current generation, more than any other, must take on the challenging work of *unseparation* to initiate an Age of Union, using everything we have created thus far, the knowledge and wisdom of generations past, and our incredibly high capacity for changemaking, to our collective advantage.

Lead from the heart and from the soul. Put in the work to connect deeply with our collective source, so that you may become an instrument for change and transformation—a beacon of light to dispel the darkness. Enact change on a behavioural level, on a daily level, and on a local level, and cultivate these changes like seedlings so they grow as tall as their roots grow deep.

We can all be changemakers; we can all dream of mending humanity's fragmented relationship with this planet. With these Acts of Union, with these conscious choices, we are building alternatives and creating new narratives. We are building a new foundation.

The time for an Age of Union is now. Let every action bring it closer into view. Let every step forward bring hope and unity. Let individuals lead in their own ways. Let there be a collective rise in consciousness. And once we fully realize this union, once we return to the garden, let us end separation and be *never apart*.

Every daily act can
be an act of elevation.

Art Curation

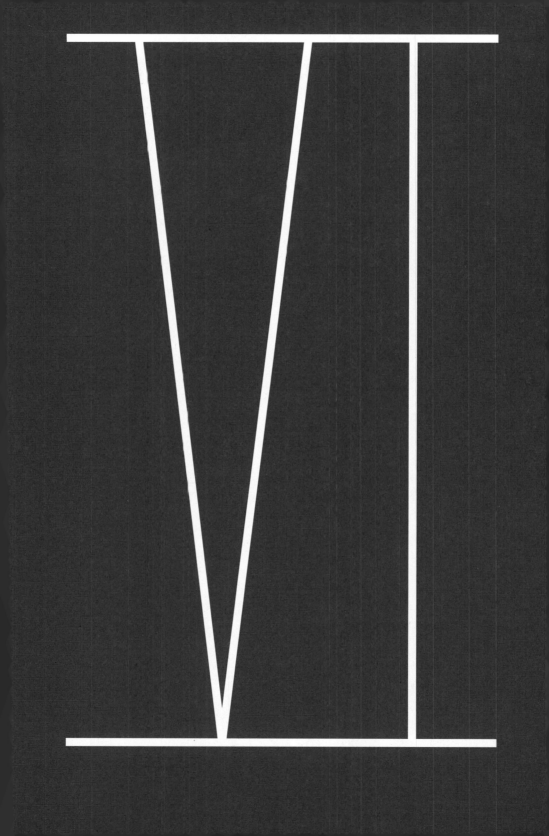

The Chromatic Age

They are part of the world, soak it in, and put themselves at risk to better feel it. Artists challenge reality, filtering the world around them through their senses, engaging in dialogue with it, and participating in its transformation. Inherently, the creative act contains an almost sacred offering that conjures togetherness.

In curating the works that appear in this book, we chose to adopt an intuitive approach over an intellectual one. An important visual component to a text already so well steeped in thought, these works of art evoke a visceral response to the world we inhabit. Through these vibrant images, we may also project our view of the world we wish to inhabit and carry this view through our experience in reading Age of Union. The works that appear in this publication thus constitute immersive spaces—a radical idea, a set of intensities, of energies, bounded by the space of this book.

Nine contemporary artists who engage in diverse practices (photography, sculpture, painting, and digital media) are represented here in a dozen key chromatic works.

You'll find spectacular disconcerting landscapes that have all been tampered with, transformed. They are representations of nature indelibly marked by the human hand—nature altered in its very essence. Each work here is, by virtue of its colour, necessarily tied to the others, creating a striking chromatic experience.

These works reflect a contemporary paradigm, marked by our era's environmental awareness. Each landscape has been altered, deserted, yet still contains memory, which evokes life. More importantly, a vibrant, gripping beauty emerges from these artificial landscapes.

Thus, this collective statement is intended to be timely and powerful. It enables the intersection of digital and physical worlds, dreams and reality, artificiality and nature, humanity and wilderness, which, far from being mere dichotomies, are in symbiosis and in constant evolution.

JEAN-SÉBASTIEN BAILLAT
Art Director and Curator

Artist Bios

BY SKY GOODDEN
AND SARA SMITH

01—REFIK ANADOL

Refik Anadol (b. 1985, Istanbul, Turkey) is a media artist, director, and pioneer in the aesthetics of machine intelligence. His body of work locates creativity at the intersection of humans and machines. In taking the data that flows around us as his primary material, and the neural network of a computerized mind as his collaborator, Anadol paints with a thinking brush, offering us radical visualizations of our digitized memories and expanding the possibilities of architecture, narrative, and the body in motion. Anadol's site-specific parametric data sculptures, live audio/visual performances, and immersive installations take many forms, offering a dramatic rethinking of the physical world, our relationship to time and space, and the creative potential of machines.

Engram: Data Sculpture, 2018, LED media wall.

02—NEIL KRUG

Neil Krug (b. 1983) is an American photographer and filmmaker based in Los Angeles. Born and raised in Kansas, Krug has often been cited as a standout in the resurgence of film experimentation within the millennial generation. Since 2009, Krug has produced artwork to accompany over 40 album campaigns (Lana Del Rey, Cage the Elephant, Unknown Mortal Orchestra), released three fine art photography books, and directed several music videos. "There has never been an exact process, per se. All I'm ever trying to do is chase the fragmented daydream images that come to me," Krug says. "Taking bits of ideas that occur in idle moments and trying to turn them into tangible imagery."

Birth, 2018, colour photograph.
The Kiss, 2018, colour photograph.
Animalia in Blue, 2018, colour photograph.

03—NIK MIRUS

Nik Mirus (b. 1981) was born in Montréal and graduated from the Dawson College Institute of Photography. Mirus, also a successful commercial photographer, shifts his focus in artistic practice to "what is left behind in our pursuit of materialistic interests." Training his camera on objects such as obsolete detritus, he works to elevate his subjects and breathe new life into the discarded. We should "question our consumerist habits as well as appreciate the importance of being able to see the beauty in the mundane and banal objects that we pass by daily," he says. Mirus has been twice-awarded the Magenta Foundation's annual photography competition, Flash Forward. He is currently based in Montréal, where he pursues both a personal artistic practice and shoots commercially for a variety of national and international clients.

Debris #1. Plastic Bag, Archival InkJet Print, 61 x 81.4 cm.

Debris #2. Broken Mirror, Archival InkJet Print, 61 x 81.4 cm.

04—BRADLEY G MUNKOWITZ

Bradley G Munkowitz (b. 1975), or GMUNK, is an artist who spans multiple media to promote a singular style, which he terms "enigmatic, atmospheric, and metaphysical." Fusing science fiction, psychedelic palettes, and graphic design, GMUNK's work presents an opportunity for escape through lush textures and light play. He maps sculpture, choreographs robots, and collaborates constantly, all in order to unify his efforts in a search for personal connection through technology. Working between kaleidoscopic abstractions and existential figuration—and across a multitude of platforms that stress accessibility—GMUNK often fragments the moving image or sets in motion that which is still. Infusing staid symbols with cinematic effect, and technology with human sensation, his "curated perspective," GMUNK says, "focuses on dramatic vantage points... It's an escape and opportunity to embrace nature through a unique lens."

Coastal Silhouette, 2018, Medium-Format Photography – printed on A2 Canson Infinity Platine Fibre Rag Paper.

Icelandic Fire, 2017, Infrared Photography – printed on A2 Canson Infinity Platine Fibre Rag Paper.

05—BENOÎT PAILLÉ

Benoît Paillé (b. 1984) has lived an itinerant life, both geographically and creatively. On the road since 2013, he now pursues art where he once pursued medicine. Of this perpetual seeking, he says, "I chose to transform my life in an attempt to transform my art." Paillé recalls a childhood of second-hand smoke, an adolescence hazed by Ritalin, and an adulthood love affair with photography. Prone to depression, and a vocal proponent of psychotropics, Paillé says he does not seek his images out, but that they appear to him spontaneously. His freedom of movement encourages these visions and has brought him to see the world through a slightly distorted lens. The banal bends to kitsch in his hands; the absurd breaks out. Paillé has renounced the dictatorship of images and works to pervert our familiar symbols. His photos are instead tableaux of objects that balance on the edge of parody.

> *Bush fire 1, Surreal Mexico series*, 2016, inkjet.

> *Bush fire 2, Surreal Mexico series*, 2016, inkjet, Hahnemühle paper.

06—TESS ROBY

Tess Roby (b. 1993) is a Toronto born, Montréal-based photographer and musician. Capturing traces of travels, Roby abstracts the urban architectural landscape of the cities she wanders in, finding sublimity in the commonplace and revealing its beauty. Shot on 35mm film, her photographs exhibit the unmistakable grain of the medium, ethereally transforming subtleties through Roby's lens. Each image holds a dreamlike quality, presenting everyday occurrences that blur visual boundaries, and creating a space which Roby describes as "cinematic, caught, and sometimes surreal."

> *Palm Through Fence, Avalon*, 2017, archival inkjet print.

07—JULIE ROCH-CUERRIER

Julie Roch-Cuerrier (b. 1988) is a Montréal-based artist who spans a range of media including printmaking, photography, installation, and sculpture. Her practice "takes form as a set of experiments in which truth and fiction are intentionally confused, in an attempt to reach an external reality." Processes of mutability and "the potential for thoughts and concepts to migrate or leak into a different state or another being" are central to her focus. Her work has been presented in numerous galleries both in Canada and internationally, including Division Gallery (Montréal), Whitechapel Gallery (London), and Biquini Wax EPS (Mexico City), among others. Roch-Cuerrier holds an M.A. in Printmaking from the Royal College of Art in London and a B.A. in Studio Arts from Concordia University in Montréal.

> *The Worm Hole*, 2015, inkjet print on archival paper.

08—FLORENCE YEE

Florence Yee (b. 1996) is a queer Cantonese artist based in Toronto and Montréal. Their interest in Cantonese-Canadian history has fuelled an art practice examining the dailiness of diaspora through the lenses of gender, racialization, queerness, and language. "I was once told that my work is a collection of purposefully bad forgeries," Yee says. Through an interdisciplinary practice comprising installation, painting, fibres, and sculpture, Yee propels a methodology of "copying, tracing, re-staging, and autobiographical re-making." They imbue culturally neglected objects with a reinvested energy and ring them with ritual. Themes of authenticity and failure trace their practice, and exercise the permutations of language, ancestry, and both cultural learning and forgetting. Yee is currently pursuing an MFA at OCAD University and is represented by Studio Sixty-Six in Ottawa.

The End Is Past, 2018, digital print on aluminum.

Perception is Nine Tenths of the Law, 2018, digital print on aluminum.

This is Not Photorealism III, 2016, oil on canvas.

09—JONATHAN ZAWADA

Jonathan Zawada (b. 1981) works in the fields of art and design, and braids digital media with an analogue approach. Rooted in coding, graphic design, and illustration, Zawada's practice is traced with the ephemera of virtual experience. His works of object and furniture design, sculpture, video, installation, and painting are centred around the intersection of the artificial and the natural. In a style that's hyperreal and delicate, he has presented solo exhibitions across Los Angeles, Paris, Tokyo, London, Sydney, and Beijing. Speaking of his entrance into contemporary art, he says simply, "I've settled on the idea that I like to make things." Zawada has been celebrated for his ability to recognize the characteristics inherent to a place or object and illuminate its essential being.

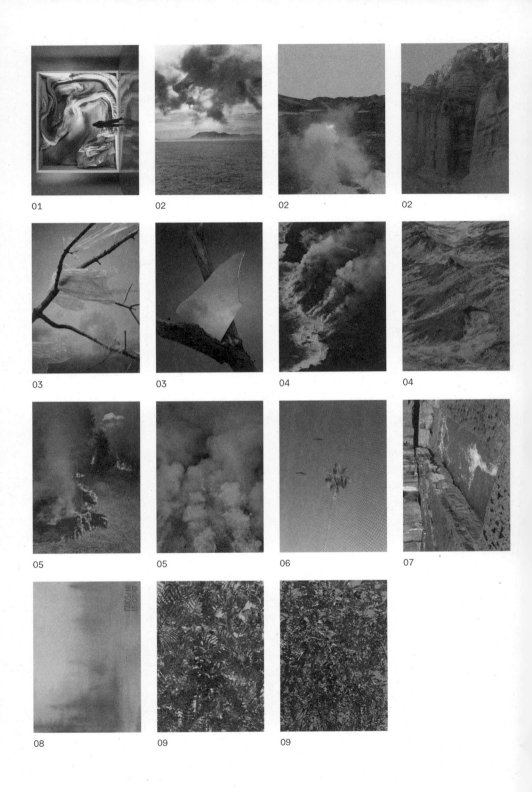

01

02

02

02

03

03

04

04

05

05

06

07

08

09

09

Age of Union

Acknowledgements

A special thank you to my family and friends for your support throughout this journey—especially my parents Anne and Joe, and my partner Nik, for being the greatest.

To *Age of Union* Editorial Director Catherine Métayer and Curator-Art Director Jean-Sébastien Baillat, I am deeply grateful. Without your vision and belief, this book would not have reached its final, physical form—a massive thank you!

Thank you, Mariette Raina, for your support throughout this process, from before the beginning to continuing the mission after the book's release. And to Harley Smart and Anteism Books for guiding the project through the world of publishing.

Thank you to all of the artists whose brilliant works appear throughout the book, and to illustrator Stéphane Poirier, who has captured *Age of Union* so beautifully in his work. Thank you to editors Jeremy Young and Sara Smith, designers Louis Dollé, Sara Thion and Capucine Labarthe, proofreaders Shanti Maharaj and Edwin Janzen, and everyone at Baillat Studio and BESIDE.

Thank you to PR masters Bradley Grill and Natasha Koifman for helping me get the word out on a project so important to me.

Thank you to Justin Kingsley and Douglas Coupland, who encouraged me as a writer and generously showed me the way.

Thank you to Rabbi Avraham Feigelstock and Rabbi Mendel Friedman for their spiritual guidance and open hearts.

And thank you to the teams at Lightspeed and Never Apart, and in particular Michael Venus, without whom there would be no journey.

@daxdasilva
www.daxdasilva.com

@lightspeedhq
www.lightspeedhq.com

@neverapartmtl
www.neverapart.com

@ageofunion
www.ageofunion.com

About the Author

DAX DASILVA
Founder & CEO, Lightspeed
Founder, Never Apart

Dax Dasilva is the creative mind behind Lightspeed, Never Apart, and *Age of Union*. Founded in 2005, Lightspeed develops a cloud commerce platform used by retail and restaurant customers in over a hundred countries. The company's mission is to bring cities and communities to life by empowering independent business.

In 2015 Dasilva also founded Never Apart, a cultural non-profit determined to bring about positive social change and unity through original programming with global reach and impact. Housed in Lightspeed's former offices, Never Apart cultivates a diverse following and has welcomed thousands into its 12,000-square-foot space.

Helping entrepreneurs become leaders in their communities through Lightspeed's technology and elevating artists through his work at Never Apart are fundamental to Dasilva's philosophy. He fosters cultures of innovation, promotes diverse leadership, and values different viewpoints.

With *Age of Union*, Dasilva brings leadership, spirituality and environmental guardianship together with themes of identity, diversity, cultural expression, and individual empowerment to ignite the impactful changemakers that the world needs now.

For the eagle, the elk,
the whale, the tusker,
the wolf, the ape, and the lion

The mother, the father, the child
The sun, the moon
The sea, the sky, and the wild

The wind, the breath of the source
The garment of flame
The robe of an ember
The dance round the fire in the forest